THE CASE OF COUCH & MEREDITH

Mark C. Anderson

couchandmeredith@gmail.com

©2013

First Edition

ISBN-13: 978-0615852096
ISBN-10: 0615852092

PREFACE

My father, J. Robert Anderson, was a great local historian.

He lived his first five years on a homestead just outside of the town of Effie, in northern Minnesota, in one of the last areas opened up for homesteading. His family moved into the town of Effie in 1928, and he lived in the area most of his life.

He grew up knowing the other people who had homesteaded in the area, who became farmers, loggers and merchants.

During the 1960s, as many of these early settlers were coming into old age, Dad bought a little Sony reel-to-reel recorder and began taking the oral histories of the rich lives of these people.

He kept a file of his recollections about the people and events of Effie.

He spent parts of three decades researching the life of an early area Indian Chief and wrote a book about him, "Chief Busticogan."

As we would travel the roads around Effie, Dad was always quick to point out who had lived where and what had taken place when.

On occasion, as we would travel east of town on Highway 1, Dad would point to a wooded area where when he was about fifteen years old the FBI had arrested two kidnappers.

As I grew older, I found that I also enjoyed researching and collecting the vast history of this area. I would recall the tidbits of history Dad had instilled in me in my youth and would ask him to expound on them.

In the early 2000s, I came in contact with Leonard Knotts, Jr., who was born in Effie in 1938, but had lived most of his life on the west coast of the United States. Len had the good fortune to purchase the log cabin in Effie in which he had been born, and he returns there from California to spend his summers.

Len is also a great local historian who has collected a lot of Effie history and is always looking for more.

Len and I traded myth and folklore about this area, as we tried to sort fact from fiction.

Whenever we had a question on some event or person, we would always turn to Dad, whose memory was lucid until the day he passed away in early 2006.

It was shortly after Dad's death that I realized I had never probed him for more information on the FBI kidnapping arrest.

I Googled "FBI Effie Kidnapping" and found nothing (well, actually way too much, but none that I was looking for).

I contacted some folks around Effie, and found several people who recalled, or had heard of the incident, and I was able to get a few names of some of the people involved. After I had this information, I was able to start my research on this case wholeheartedly, and I spent the next several years unraveling the story.

What I found was that the kidnapping was actually the last of many crimes in a spree that had begun a few weeks earlier by a couple of young men from St. Louis who had earlier spent time together in prison.

I examined files from the US National Archives and old newspaper clippings. I contacted relatives of the principal people involved. I was able to get the FBI report on the case. I received help from libraries and historians. I met many great people along the way.

I basically had to turn over every rock that I could find to flesh out this story more. New pieces of information would give me clues as to what to look for next. As I proceeded, I was amazed at the twists and turns this story took. I decided that this should all be put into a book, in spite of the fact that I had never written a book before.

I want this book to be an accurate record of what transpired, as best as it can be so many years after the fact. Any statement in quotation marks is documented as having been spoken by that person. Documents included are italicized and are presented exactly as they were written (and yes, "kidnaping" with one "p" was the proper spelling at that time). Jack Meredith used many variations of his name throughout his lifetime, so you will see them change as the story progresses.

Many of the pictures included are of poor quality, but they are the best that can be found.

I have made the decision to include some names, addresses, and other minutiae, which will mean nothing to most readers. It is my hope that they might catch someone's attention who may be able to add more to this great story.

Enjoy the ride!

Mark Anderson

James Otis Meredith lies on the examination table of a small town doctor's office. Several buckshot have penetrated his lower back, as has a .32 caliber bullet.

A Federal Agent stands by Meredith's side, as Dr. Bender works on his wounds.

"It's a losing game. You can't win," Meredith says to the agent, "I'm done for."

Dr. Bender tells Meredith that he might not be hurt that badly.

Meredith says that he wished he had been hit higher, "so that it might be all over now."

Dr. Bender tries to reassure him of some hope, but Meredith replies, "No, I can feel it moving towards my heart..."

James Otis Meredith

JAMES OTIS MEREDITH

James Otis Meredith was born to Grace and James Thomas Meredith on June 30, 1912, in Glenwood, Arkansas. He had an older brother, William Alfred, or "Al," who was born in 1910.

James Thomas and Grace divorced around 1915. James moved to Texas, where he remarried a few years later and started a new family. Grace and the two boys moved in with her parents, James and Louella Cockrell. Grace took a job as a waitress.

Al and James Otis, or "Otie" as the family called him, also lived with their Meredith grandparents for a while.

On June 2, 1916, Grace married Jess Sellers. They remained in southern Arkansas. Young James took on the name Otis Sellers, and his brother, Alfred Sellers.

Grace and Jess had a son, Leon, who was born in August of 1917. Their daughter Geraldine was born in June of 1919.

Jess was very strict with the children, and Al and Otie did not get along with him very well.

Grace divorced Jess Sellers on November 10, 1925.

Otis was a pleasant and charismatic lad, but in his teen years he started getting into trouble with the law.

On July 10, 1929, 17 year-old Otis Sellers was convicted on charges of burglary and larceny and was sentenced to serve five years in the Missouri State Penitentiary in Jefferson City.

Meredith worked as a machine operator in a clothing factory in the penitentiary.

On September 20, 1930, Otis Sellers was paroled by Governor Henry S. Caulfield.

On October 26, 1930, Otis was arrested for attempted robbery and was sentenced to serve five years at the State

Reformatory in Boonville, Missouri. He escaped from custody on December 29th.

February 26, 1931, Otis was arrested for auto theft and he was returned to the Boonville Reformatory.

After being released from Boonville, Otis enrolled in the Civilian Conservation Corps. In November 1933 Meredith was sent to the Deer Lake CCC Camp outside of the town of Effie in northern Minnesota. He signed on as "John Meredith" but went by the name of "Jack." He was in Co. #1763, which had completed the construction of this camp, and was now assigned to work in the George Washington State Forest.

Meredith was 5' 11", about 160 lbs., with dark wavy chestnut hair and hazel eyes. He was of fair complexion and of medium slender build. He had the initials "JOS" tattooed in blue on his left outer forearm and the word "Mother" in a heart on his right inner forearm. He also had a cross, outlined in blue on his right upper arm.

Meredith had only a fifth grade education, but he was quite well spoken and very personable. He played guitar and loved music.

Jack loved Minnesota's northwoods, and spent much of his free time fishing the many area lakes.

Charles Rootes, a local, was employed at the Deer Lake CCC camp.

Originally from Michigan, Charles made his home a few miles from the camp on a farm with his wife Gladys and their children who were still living at home: Roy (who was also working at he CCC Camp) and his wife Doris, Vera, Luther, Lloyd, Carl and Raymond. Charles' other daughters, Ida and Beatrice, had moved away from home by this time

Jack Meredith met Charles' daughter, Vera, and they courted.

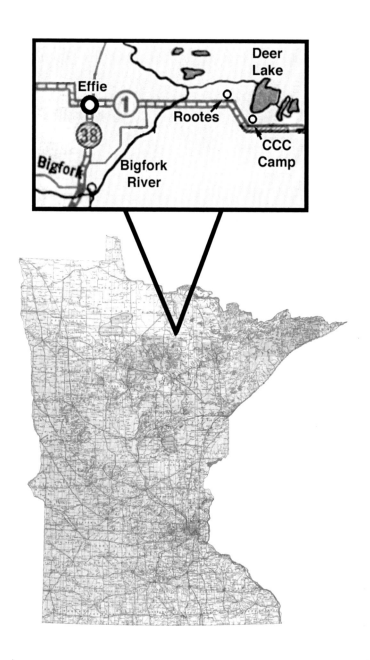

Jack and Vera
1934

Meredith was honorably discharged from the CCC on March 31, 1934.

On April 5, 1934, Vera married John Otis Meredith in front of a Justice of the Peace in Grand Rapids, Minnesota. She was 16 and he was 21.

Vera gave birth to Deloris Marie Meredith on January 2, 1935.

The Merediths moved to Minneapolis and rented a place at a rooming house at 2801 Portland Avenue. Jack got a job in Minneapolis working as a punch craftsman for William Bros Boiler and Manufacturing on Nicollet Island.

In May of 1936, they moved to St. Louis. They moved in with Meredith's mother, who was now known as Grace O'Neal.

Vera and Jack were not getting along, and after a short time in St. Louis, Vera and Deloris left Jack, and returned to Minnesota in June.

Vera found a job in Minneapolis, working for her friend Mrs. Bieker in a rest home. Eventually, she and Deloris returned home to her parent's farm near Effie.

In 1937, Jack got a job as a salesman at the Union May Stern Company, a furniture store at Olive and Twelfth Street in St. Louis.

On May 20, 1938, there was a shortage discovered in Meredith's accounts at the Union May Stern Company and he was discharged.

Meredith looked for new employment, but not very diligently. Grace feared that Otis might return to crime and pressured him to find work.

Jack spent a lot of his free time around the area of Taylor and Page in St. Louis. He frequented Thomas' Liquors at 1233 North Taylor and also Jim's Café, a restaurant and tavern diagonally across the block from Thomas' at 4503 Page.

On the evening of Tuesday, July 19, 1938, Jack encountered John Couch at Jim's Café. Jack and John had spent time together at the Reformatory in Boonville.

John Couch

JOHN COUCH

John Couch was born September 3, 1915, in St. Louis, Missouri, to John William Couch (who goes by the name William) and Rose Etta Johnson Couch. John had three brothers, Andrew Levi (16), Russell William (12), and George Thomas (8); and two sisters, Frances Mary (3), and Dorothy Eugenia (1-1/2).

William Couch was a skilled tradesman, and was able to provide adequately for his family.

Rose Etta and William Couch

In 1918, William Couch lost a leg in an automobile accident. He received $3,000 in compensation but was unable to continue his skilled trade and became a laborer. He started to drink heavily. Their home life was not harmonious, and they were living in poverty. They were living in a rental at 1211 Hickory in St. Louis.

In 1919, Andrew Levi Couch married Edna Brauer.

In 1920, George Thomas Couch, 13, was sent to the Belle Fontaine Boys Home on some charge.

In 1926, 10 year-old John Couch was arrested for the first time, for the theft of a bicycle. He was given probation.

John Couch 1926

John was subsequently arrested several times for other minor offenses and was given "Bench Parole" each time.

In 1927, at age 12, John Couch took a job as a paperboy to help his family out. They were now living at 3832 West Pine Street, St. Louis.

That same year, Frances Mary Couch married 21-year-old Carl Tilden Whitter. She was only 15 at the time, but her Mother vouched on her marriage application that she was 17.

In 1928, Dorothy Eugenia Couch, 14, married Arthur William Whitter, 17, (Carl's brother).

On Valentine's Day in 1928, 13-year old John Couch was arrested in St. Louis for purse snatching. He was committed to Belle Fontaine Boys Home. He was treated well there but escaped because he was homesick. When he was recaptured, he was sent to serve two years at the Reformatory in Boonville, Missouri.

Couch claimed that while at the Boonville Reformatory he was abused and regularly beaten. He claimed that records would show that several of the boys had been beaten to death. In his words, "The smaller the boy, the more beatings he received."

On September 18, 1929, John's devoted mother, Rose Etta Johnson Couch, died at home of Carcinoma. William Couch's cousin, Dr. Leo B. Couch, attended her.

John Couch was given a furlough due to his mother's illness. He was later given a discharge without having to report back.

December 16, 1929, John Couch was arrested on burglary and attempted larceny charges and was sentenced to serve two years in the State Reformatory at Boonville.

In 1930, Andrew Couch divorced Edna and was living with his father, along with Dorothy and Arthur Whitter, at 919 North Taylor in St. Louis. Dorothy worked as a dietician

John Couch

at Missouri Baptist Hospital at Taylor and Hedeman Avenue in St. Louis where her father William also worked as a maintenance man. Andrew worked as a blacksmith, and Arthur was employed as a cabinetmaker.

In 1931, John Couch made a couple of escapes from the reformatory but was quickly recaptured each time. He stole an automobile each time he was free and was subsequently sentenced to remain in the Boonville Reformatory until he reached the age of 21.

January 10, 1932, John Couch escaped from the House of Detention, at 14th & Clark in St. Louis, while awaiting removal to the Reformatory on the charge of auto theft. In affecting his escape, he assaulted guard Edward Spinder with a 10" iron spindle bolt, causing great injury. Couch was recaptured February 7th.

John Couch completed the 6th grade in the reformatory, after having failed it twice.

November 30, 1932, John Couch escaped from the State Reformatory in Boonville. He was recaptured the same day and was delivered back to the Reformatory.

May 16, 1933, John Couch again escaped from Boonville and stole a car but was recaptured the same day.

He was sentenced to serve nine years in the State Prison in Jefferson City, Missouri.

Couch stated that while in the State Prison, "They put bitterness and hatred in my heart."

He claimed to have spent three years in solitary confinement, which he said permanently embittered him.

Over the term of his incarcerations, Couch worked in a shoe factory, an overall factory, and did some quarry work.

April 29, 1934, St. Louis Police Officer Albert Siko was shot while breaking up a streetcar robbery. Other officers trapped a suspect, Louis De More, in an alley. De More was positively identified by the wounded officer and the streetcar driver, Thomas Foster.

De More pled guilty.

Siko died from his injuries a few days later.

May 13, 1934, Police executed a search warrant on George Couch and found the slain officer's pistol in his possession.

George claimed that he found the gun, but Russell Couch told the officers that George brought it home one day, saying that he had just, "shot it out with a cop."

Louis De More pled his innocence to Governor Guy B. Clark, saying that he only pled guilty because he was told he would hang if found guilty by a jury. Governor Clark granted him a full pardon.

George Couch was put on trial for the murder of Albert Siko, and found guilty, but his trial was dismissed because of two technical errors. His second and third trials ended in hung juries, but he was convicted again on his fourth. He was sent to serve a life term at the State Prison in Jefferson City, Missouri. His life sentence was affirmed on appeal to the Missouri Supreme Court in 1937.

January

Su	Mo	Tu	We	Th	Fr	Sa
						1
2	3	4	5	6	7	8
9	10	11	12	13	14	15
16	17	18	19	20	21	22
23	24	25	26	27	28	29
30	31					

1:● 9:◑ 16:○ 23:◐ 31:●

February

Su	Mo	Tu	We	Th	Fr	Sa
		1	2	3	4	5
6	7	8	9	10	11	12
13	14	15	16	17	18	19
20	21	22	23	24	25	26
27	28					

7:◑ 14:○ 21:◐

March

Su	Mo	Tu	We	Th	Fr	Sa
		1	2	3	4	5
6	7	8	9	10	11	12
13	14	15	16	17	18	19
20	21	22	23	24	25	26
27	28	29	30	31		

2:● 9:◑ 16:○ 23:◐ 31:●

April

Su	Mo	Tu	We	Th	Fr	Sa
					1	2
3	4	5	6	7	8	9
10	11	12	13	14	15	16
17	18	19	20	21	22	23
24	25	26	27	28	29	30

7:◑ 14:○ 22:◐ 30:●

May

Su	Mo	Tu	We	Th	Fr	Sa
1	2	3	4	5	6	7
8	9	10	11	12	13	14
15	16	17	18	19	20	21
22	23	24	25	26	27	28
29	30	31				

6:◑ 14:○ 22:◐ 29:●

June

Su	Mo	Tu	We	Th	Fr	Sa
			1	2	3	4
5	6	7	8	9	10	11
12	13	14	15	16	17	18
19	20	21	22	23	24	25
26	27	28	29	30		

5:◑ 12:○ 20:◐ 27:●

July

Su	Mo	Tu	We	Th	Fr	Sa
					1	2
3	4	5	6	7	8	9
10	11	12	13	14	15	16
17	18	19	20	21	22	23
24	25	26	27	28	29	30
31						

4:◑ 12:○ 20:◐ 26:●

August

Su	Mo	Tu	We	Th	Fr	Sa
	1	2	3	4	5	6
7	8	9	10	11	12	13
14	15	16	17	18	19	20
21	22	23	24	25	26	27
28	29	30	31			

2:◑ 11:○ 18:◐ 25:●

September

Su	Mo	Tu	We	Th	Fr	Sa
				1	2	3
4	5	6	7	8	9	10
11	12	13	14	15	16	17
18	19	20	21	22	23	24
25	26	27	28	29	30	

1:◑ 9:○ 16:◐ 23:●

October

Su	Mo	Tu	We	Th	Fr	Sa
						1
2	3	4	5	6	7	8
9	10	11	12	13	14	15
16	17	18	19	20	21	22
23	24	25	26	27	28	29
30	31					

1:◑ 9:○ 16:◐ 23:● 31:◑

November

Su	Mo	Tu	We	Th	Fr	Sa
		1	2	3	4	5
6	7	8	9	10	11	12
13	14	15	16	17	18	19
20	21	22	23	24	25	26
27	28	29	30			

7:○ 14:◐ 21:● 29:◑

December

Su	Mo	Tu	We	Th	Fr	Sa
				1	2	3
4	5	6	7	8	9	10
11	12	13	14	15	16	17
18	19	20	21	22	23	24
25	26	27	28	29	30	31

7:○ 13:◐ 21:● 29:◑

1938

1938

Franklin D. Roosevelt was President of the United States.

Following a number of years of economic improvement during the depression, a recession hits the country, bringing unemployment back up to around 19%, from 14% in 1937, and the average income dropped from $1,780 the year before, to $1,730.

Robberies and kidnappings often made the headlines in the papers, as some of the population was desperate enough to get some money anyway that they could.

Gasoline cost 10¢ a gallon, bread 9¢ a loaf, and a first class postage stamp was 3¢. An average new car went for about $736.

Oil was discovered in Kuwait, transforming the Emirate's economy.

Evel Knievel, Ted Turner, Christopher Lloyd, Wolfman Jack, Etta James, Kofi Annan, Duane Eddy, Peter Jennings, and Pat Buchanan were all born this year.

Teflon, Nylon, Xerography, freeze dried coffee, and the ballpoint pen were invented.

Superman made his debut in the comics, and an early version of Bugs Bunny appeared in "Porky's Hare Hunt."

The New York Yankees beat the Chicago Cubs 4-0 in the World Series.

Racehorse Seabiscuit defeated War Admiral at Pimlico in the "Match of the Century."

Joe Louis knocked out Germany's Max Schmeling for the World Heavyweight Boxing Championship.

Thornton Wilder's "Our Town" made its stage debut.

Artie Shaw's "Begin the Beguine" was the highest charting song of the year.

Kate Smith sang "God Bless America" for the first time, on her radio show on the day before Armistice Day. Orson Welles broadcast his adaptation of H.G. Wells' "War of the Worlds" on the night before Halloween. The broadcast caused panic nationwide as many believed that aliens had actually landed in New Jersey.

Filming began on the "Wizard of Oz."

Disney released "Snow White and the Seven Dwarfs." Other films released were "A Christmas Carol," "Room Service" with the Marx Brothers, "Bringing up Baby," "Boys Town," "Jezebel" and "Pygmalion."

Frank Capra's "You Can't Take It With You" was the number one film of the year.

Hal Roach Studios temporarily replaced Stan Laurel, of the "Laurel & Hardy" team, with Harold Langdon in the film "Zenobia's Infidelity" over a contract dispute.

Daniel Dodge, heir to the Dodge Motor fortune, died from wounds he received playing with dynamite at his vacation home on an island in Canada, while on his honeymoon.

"Wrong Way" Corrigan took off from New York in his plane, ostensibly heading for California, but "accidentally" landed in Ireland instead.

Siam was officially renamed Thailand.

A hurricane hit Long Island, leaving 63,000 people homeless, and 700 dead.

The Nazis began "Kristallnacht" on November 9th.

Adolph Hitler was Time Magazine's "Man of the Year."

April 30, 1938

Floyd Hamilton, Huron Ted Walters and Irvin Goodspeed escaped from the Montague County Texas Jail.

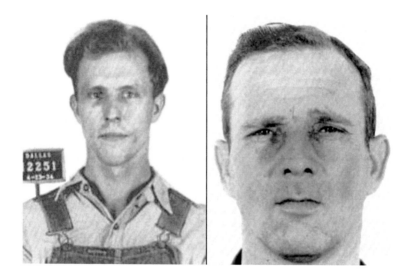

Floyd Hamilton   **Huron Ted Walters**

Hamilton and Walters were being held in the small Texas jail on an auto theft charge.

Hamilton was a minor player in the Barrow/Parker gang of "Bonnie and Clyde" fame. Floyd's brother Raymond was a bigger player in that gang, and had been executed in the electric chair in 1935 for his criminal activities.

Hamilton feared that if he were convicted, he would be sent to Huntsville Prison, where he believed the Warden there had it out for him.

On an evening when Kenneth Chandler was the only guard on duty, the three men overpowered him. Goodspeed stabbed Chandler in the leg with scissors to keep him from following them.

Chandler's Mother, Mrs. H. T. Chandler, was the Sheriff of Montague County. She had been appointed to the office several months earlier after the death of her husband.

Goodspeed parted company with Hamilton and Walters soon after the break.

May 3, 1938

Irvin Goodspeed was recaptured without resistance at Nocona, Texas. He denied having any information concerning Hamilton and Walters.

Irvin Goodspeed after his recapture

May 26, 1938

Hamilton and Walters escaped law officers in a running gun battle near Tyler, Texas.

June 7, 1938

Hamilton and Walters, along with wheelman Jack Winn, robbed the Bank of Bradley, Arkansas. They got away with $685.

June 16, 1938

John Couch was given parole on conditional release by Missouri Governor Lloyd C. Stark.

John Couch was now 22 years old, 5' 7" tall, and weighed about 150 lbs. He had brown eyes and dark brown hair, and a dark ruddy complexion.

Upon Couch's return home from the state penitentiary, he found his father in a saloon in St. Louis with a "chippy." William acted as if he did not know John.

Couch was told by his Parole Officer that there would be a job for him in St. Louis. However, when he arrived there, he was told that his job had been taken by someone else. He went to his parole officer twice more, trying to find work, but was told that they could not help him get a job.

July 19, 1938

Tuesday

John Couch went out for a couple of beers at Jim's Café, at Taylor and Page in St. Louis. Jim's was operated by Greek immigrant James Louis, and his German wife Molly. The café is housed in the same building as Dentist Kalmun Kramer, and Physician Henry Rosenberg. Wayne Babcock's filling station is just across the intersection to the east. To the southeast is Thomas' Liquors, and there is another restaurant to the southwest, which is run by Frank Robert.

At Jim's Cafe, Couch ran into Jack Meredith, with whom he had spent time earlier in the decade in incarceration.

July 21, 1938

Thursday

John Couch and his brother Russell go to Jim's Café.

Jack Meredith is there again, and he asks John whether or not he has had any luck in finding work.

John replies that he hasn't.

Jack has not found work yet either, and he suggests to John that he might have a plan to make a little money.

Couch is interested and Meredith explains that he has a car, and they could take a road trip, and that they could hit up some small establishments when they needed some cash.

Russell Couch hears of the plan and interjects that John is just out of prison and on parole, and it would be wise for him to keep away from any trouble.

Meredith goes back to his table and after a while he motions Couch to join him.

Jack tells John to think about his plan, and if he is still interested, they should meet up again without Russell.

Couch says that he will meet Meredith at Jim's on Sunday night.

July 24, 1938

Sunday

Couch and Meredith meet as planned at the tavern.

Jack takes John outside to his 1935 Ford Tudor sedan and shows him a .38 caliber Smith and Wesson blue steel revolver.

Meredith explains that he has been arguing with his mother and he is ready to leave town.

Couch agrees to go with Meredith and mentions that Jimmy Reed would probably be willing to join them.

James Clyde Reed had spent time in incarceration with both Couch and Meredith.

1935 Ford Tudor

July 25, 1938

Monday

Couch and Meredith go to Jimmy Reed's house at 4119 Evans Avenue in St. Louis. When they get there, Couch asks Reed if he wants to leave St. Louis.

Reed asks them where they are going and they explain their plan to him.

Reed inquires if the Ford is stolen, and Meredith replies that he owns the vehicle.

Reed agrees to go along, and Couch and Meredith wait outside as he gathers some things to take with him.

James Clyde Reed is 26 years old, 5' 10-1/2" tall, 155 lbs., medium build, brown eyes, dark brown hair, and of medium complexion.

They leave St. Louis and make a stop at St. Charles, Missouri. Meredith goes into a house where an acquaintance of his lives. He returns to the car with two .32 caliber pistols.

JAMES CLYDE REED

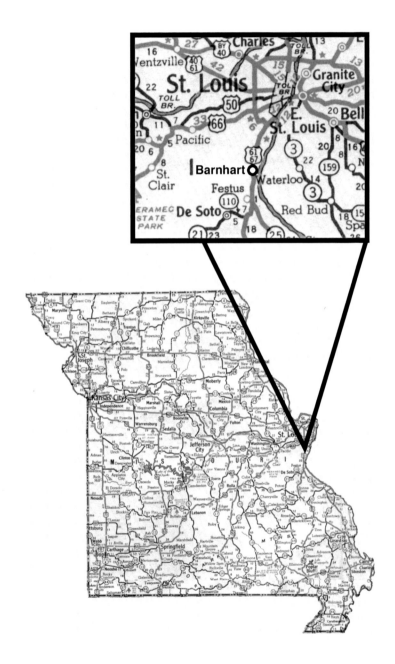

July 27, 1938

Wednesday

4:00 a.m.

Three men drive into the new Motogas filling station just south of Barnhart, Missouri, about twenty miles south of St. Louis on Highway 61. This filling station has been open only a couple of weeks. They buy three gallons of gas.

The men return to the Motogas about fifteen minutes later and have the night attendant, August Sauer, put three more gallons of gas into the car.

As August proceeds to service the car, one of the men exits the vehicle and pulls a revolver on him.

August is led back into the station and forced onto the concrete floor. His hands and feet are bound with insulated wire.

The men search August and take all of the money in his pockets, as well as taking his coin changer. They get a total of $33.40.

They cover August's head with his wool sweater while they search the premises for more money, but they find none. They repeatedly threaten Sauer with shouts of, "If you don't tell us where the rest of the money is, we will plug you."

August tells them that Ralph Warne, the manager, had been by around 2:00 a.m. and had collected most of the cash and dropped it in a night deposit at a nearby bank.

The three men search the place again. Finding nothing more, they rip the telephone off of the wall and take a radio before leaving and closing the door on Sauer.

August is able to crawl across the room on his stomach over to some boxes, which he uses to get up on his feet.

He is able to open the door and hobble over to Adolph Hemme, Sr.'s store next door, where he calls out for help.

Mr. Hemme hears his pleas, and rushes out to free Sauer from his bindings.

August Sauer quits his job following the robbery stating that he can no longer work the night shift.

July 29, 1938

Friday

The Big Chief Cabin Hotel on Highway 50 in Pond, Missouri, 25 miles west of St. Louis, is held up by three men. (Highway 50 was a very early portion of Route 66, which has now been re-routed further to the south).

They rob the filling station attendant of $25. They force him to lie on the floor and bind him with wire.

As with the MotoGas holdup two days earlier, the bandits were never identified.

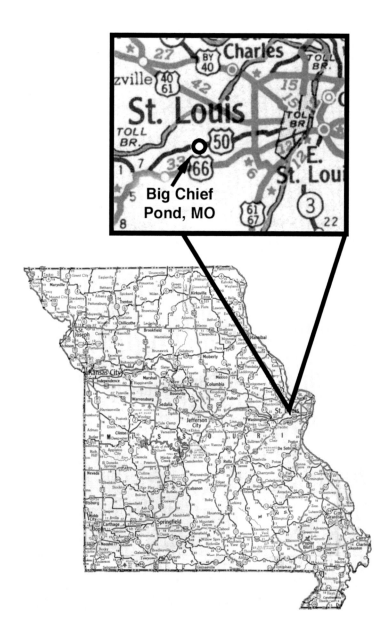

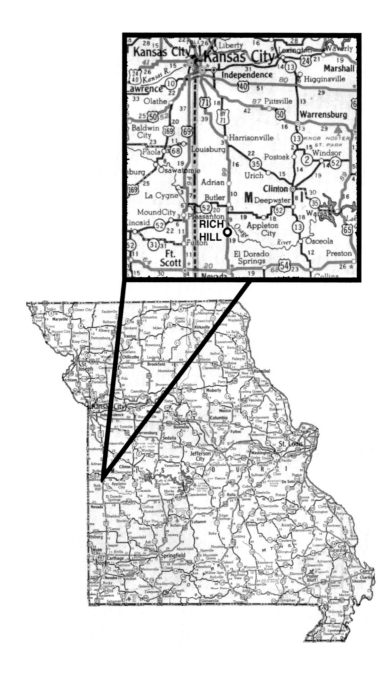

July 30, 1938

Saturday

A series of robberies take place in western Missouri, around the Kansas City area.

11:00 p.m.

Three men pull into the Skelly Filling Station just south of Rich Hill, Missouri. They purchase some gas and oil from the attendant, Elmer McKinney. Before he completes servicing the car, one of the men draws a revolver on McKinney and orders him into the station.

McKinney is told to lie on the floor. The men empty the cash register, and take what money he has in his pockets, for a total of about $50. The men grab the stock of candy and cigarettes as well.

McKinney is ordered to walk to a room at the rear of the station where he is secured with insulated wire to a bed. The men ask him if there is any more money hidden. When he replies, "No," one of the men hits him with the butt of the revolver. The men inquire about any hidden money several more times, and each time that McKinney responds that there isn't any, he is hit again with the gun. The last of these blows knocks him out.

When McKinney regains consciousness, he finds that the place has been ransacked.

It takes McKinney some time to release himself. His hands and legs have been tightly wired to the bed, and there is also a wire around his neck.

He manages to crawl to the highway to look for help.

Boyd Duffy is on his way to his home south of Rich Hill when he hears McKinney's pleas for help.

Duffy brings him back to Rich Hill, where they notify law enforcement.

McKinney recalls that the license number of the robbers' vehicle was 1938 MO 424-625 or 424-825.

July 31, 1938

Sunday

1:30 a.m.

The filling station next to the Red Onion Café in Harrisonville, Missouri, is held up by three men. Robert Arnold, the filling station attendant, is robbed and beaten.

**Filling Station and Red Onion Café
Harrisonville, Missouri**

While one of the men stays behind to guard Arnold, the other two go into the Red Onion Café next door.

Inside the Red Onion are the proprietors Curtis and Ruth Barry, Counter Man Melvin Scott, patrons Paul Simmons, Helen Spaulding, Olene Waldburger, Jim Black, Georgia Bradshaw, Dorothy Scott, Ray Anderson, A.T. Richardson, Ralph Helt, Wayne Hopkins, Charles Crager, James Perryman, Claude Harms and several others.

Curtis Barry recalled the incident in his personal memoirs:

A Sunday morning just after midnight, about 1:30 a.m., July 30th, 1938. There are about ten couples still dancing to the jukebox, and about fifteen others just sitting around and visiting. We had most everything cleaned up. Most everyone was set to go home.

I had just checked the register, only leaving a small amount of change, and a couple of dollar bills. My Wife,

Ruth, had just taken our son Charles out the back to the car. The car was parked next to the building at the west end of the restaurant. I still had my apron and chef's cap on. I was standing in the doorway to the kitchen when two young men came in the front door. One had a hand gun, and the other had a sawed off shot gun. The one with the hand gun came straight to me and said, "On the floor, this is a hold up. Everyone on the floor." I just fell backwards to the floor. My Wife, who was standing back in the kitchen said, "What's the matter Curtis?" I said, "It's a holdup."

The man with the shotgun was waving the gun, "Everyone on the floor, and stay down, and you won't get hurt."

The one with the handgun stepped behind the counter and hit Scotty, the bartender over the head, "I said down on the floor." Down he went, with the blood all over his face.

The man opened the cash register. "What, just change?"

I said, "That's all there is. The boss checked up about thirty minutes ago and had gone home."

"Where did he hide the money," was his reply.

I said, "He took it with him. That's all, take it and leave please."

"Where's your gun?" he asked.

I said "We do not have a gun. The boss said it would only get someone killed, and the robber would have another gun."

As I was lying on the floor on my back when the man stepped behind the counter, I slipped my billfold from my pocket, and slid it under the sandwich counter, which was about six inches off the floor.

Ruth and Curtis Barry
Proprietors of the Red Onion Café

In the meantime, my wife slipped out the back door to check on Charles, our son, when she ran into a man on the outside with a gun. He said, "Get back in the café." He was on the outside as a lookout. We did not know that there was three.

Chicken and Steak Dinners   Open Day and Night
Sandwiches—Short Orders   Home Cooking
Parties by Appointment

RED ONION CAFE

40 Miles South of Kansas City on Highways 71 - 35
CURTIS BERRY   Telephone 67x6
Proprietor   (Over)   Harrisonville, Mo.
364A —   *442*

THE HOUSE BY THE SIDE OF THE ROAD

Let me live in a house by the side of the road,
   Where the race of men go by—
The men who are good and the men who are bad,
   As good and as bad as I.
I would not sit in the scorner's seat,
   Or hurl the cynic's ban;—
Let me live in a house by the side of the road
   And be a friend to man.

Red Onion Café Business Card

The man with the handgun went through everyone's pockets, taking what they had. When he checked my pockets, he said, "No money?" I said, "No, I'm the cook, I don't have any money."

About that time, a man looked in at the window from the dining room to the kitchen, and said, "What's going on?"

My wife raised up on her elbows, and said, "It's a holdup. Get out a back window and go for help."

Then the man raised up the sawed-off shotgun and said, "It sure is."

My Wife just melted back to the floor.

When the man with the handgun said, "Where are the keys to the new Chevrolet?"

I said, "The man that owns it has gone with a group to the Lonesome Robin beer and dance tavern south of Freeman, Missouri. They won't be back for an hour or more."

Our car was parked in front of this new car. My Wife had the keys to our car. When she heard him say, "Where are the keys to the Chevrolet," she threw her keys in the soap chip can, which was near her. The chips were light, and the keys sunk down in them.

A young man, Jim Black, said, "Here's my keys to the Ford Coupe. Take it, and get going."

A man just inside of the dining room on the floor raised up to look around. He didn't notice the man standing just behind him. The man was the one with the shotgun. He just stepped on his head, and said, "On the floor, or I'll kill you."

About 1:45 a.m., a car pulled up in front of the café with three people in it. Mr. Bradley (Kenneth Bradley of Cleveland, Missouri) was the one that owned the car. As they were getting out, the man with the gun as a lookout met them, and marched them in the restaurant, and said, "Down on the floor with the others."

Mr. Bradley and his friends were just returning from a big dance north of Pleasant Hill, Missouri. It didn't make any difference where anyone went, they always returned to the Red Onion before going home, would order their breakfast or a sandwich. Mostly ham, bacon, or sausage; and eggs, with hashbrowns potatoes.

The man that was the lookout called in and said, "I've got a car, and filled it with gas. Come on, let's get going. You know by now that the law has found out what we did at Rich Hill."

The man with the shotgun said, "Let's take a couple of women."

The other said, "All you think about is women. We have other things to think of now." He added, "Everyone stay where you are for ten minutes, or I will kill you."

[Author's note: From their personalities, I assume that Meredith was standing lookout, Couch had the handgun, and hit Scotty, and Jimmy had the sawed-off shotgun and wanted to take some women along.]

As soon as I heard the car take off, I ran over to the filling station, but they had pulled the phone loose, and off the wall. They had also robbed the station.

I heard a moaning sound coming from the restroom. I opened the door. There lay Mr. Robert Arnold. They knocked him out, and threw him in the restroom. They had taken about $100.00 from the station.

About that time the law drove up. While talking, they noticed a fire about a quarter mile west. They hurried to the fire. The robbers had drove a car out in this field, and set it afire, making it look like they had missed the curve. That way, if the law should stop and check, it would give them more time.

•••

Shortly after 2:00 a.m. on Missouri Highway 35 just north of Harrisonville, a 1935 Ford V8 Coach is discovered burning. This vehicle is registered to J. Meredith of 59112 Degiverville Avenue, St. Louis. Some papers belonging to Meredith are found unburned in the car. This is the first time that the gang has left evidence behind which could identify any of them.

Couch, Meredith and Reed continue north on Highway 35 for about five miles before burning the rods out of Bradley's car. They set up a barricade and stop the cars of Frank Bush of Independence, Missouri, and Frank Hatton of

Pleasant Hill, Missouri, each approaching from opposite directions.

They take the Hatton car and continue north on Highway 35.

Just outside of Greenwood, Missouri, Meredith runs the Hatton car off the road and damages the rear end. They work to get the car out of the ditch but are unsuccessful.

They take their baggage out of the vehicle, remove the license plates, and set the car afire.

Around 3:00 a.m., they see another car coming towards them. They attempt to hail it, but it drives past them and pulls into the next driveway down the road.

Seventeen year-old Robert Kalousek of Greenwood is getting home late. He, his mother and a girlfriend from Lee's Summit, Missouri, had driven to Kansas City's Union Station to meet his father, who had arrived on a midnight train.

After dropping his parents off at home, Robert drove his girlfriend back to Lee's Summit, and is just now returning home.

Couch wants to get this car, but Meredith and Reed want to wait for something else to come along.

Couch points out that the burning vehicle in the ditch will probably attract some attention, and that he intends to get this other car before the authorities come around.

Couch walks up to the Kalousek home, and puts his pistol into the back of Robert Kalousek, who is just getting out of the Buick Sedan.

"Don't get excited, I only want your automobile," Couch says, "Just get in the back seat, and I won't harm you."

Kalousek gets into the back seat and Couch drives the car to where Meredith and Reed are.

Kalousek Home
Greenwood, Missouri

Couch asks the boy who he is, and he replies that he is Robert Kalousek. He adds that his father has connections in the Sheriff's Department.

When they get to Meredith and Reed, John gets out of the driver's seat and tells Meredith to drive. They load their gear into the Buick and take off.

Robert's parents hear the commotion, but by the time they get outside, they just see the taillights of their car heading down the road.

Meredith, Couch and Reed spend the rest of the night driving Robert Kalousek around the back roads east of Kansas City, Missouri.

Robert Kalousek

Couch chides Robert about whether or not he is any good with a pistol.

"I can shoot a gun." he replies.

Around 5:30 a.m., they pull the car over near the farm of David Krose, who lives in the Grand River bottoms, northeast of Carrollton, Missouri, and let Kalousek shoot the .38 pistol. Both Meredith and Reed have their guns trained on him while he handles the firearm. Robert fires the revolver once, and Couch takes the gun back from him.

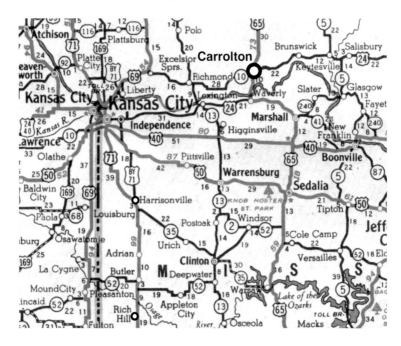

They remain here, relaxing and shooting at various targets with their guns. They leave just before noon.

They spend the rest of the afternoon criss-crossing the back roads of the area. With great luck, they evade the numerous patrols in the area out looking for them.

Around 2:00 p.m., Meredith accidentally runs the car into a ditch near Carrollton, Missouri. They are able to push the car out of the ditch and make a quick getaway, but they have been noticed.

They head towards Boonville, Missouri. On the way, Kalousek asks what they are going to do with him.

Reed and Couch tell him they are going to tie him up somewhere where he will be found in the morning.

Kalousek requests some whiskey and soda to help him get some sleep, so Jimmy Reed buys him a bottle of each at a drugstore in Boonville. Robert drinks part of the half pint of whiskey and all of the soda.

Around 11:00 p.m., they drive Kalousek out to a rock quarry about three miles from the Boonville Reformatory. They know from their stay at this reformatory that some of the inmates are brought here to work each morning, and that they will find Robert.

They take Kalousek out of the car, walk him over to the grass at the side of the road, and Couch binds his hands and feet with an electrical extension cord.

They tell Robert that they will leave his car on 18th Street in Kansas City.

The bid goodbye to Robert and continue on in his car, a 1934 black Buick Sedan, Model 57, with Missouri license 322-455.

In the morning, Kalousek is found and released from his bondage.

Robert tells the police that his kidnappers carried four revolvers and a sawed off shotgun.

Police think that two of the robbers may be Floyd Hamilton and Huron Ted Walters, who have criss-crossed the southwest with a trail of holdups since they broke out of Montague County, Texas, jail in April.

August 1, 1938

Monday

Jewell Wheeler, who lives 3-1/2 miles south of Avalon, Missouri, calls in a report to the Sheriff's office that the battery and license plates had been stolen from his car overnight. His chauffeur's license is also missing.

It is assumed that these were taken by the three men who had kidnapped Kalousek, as it is known that they had been in vicinity the night before.

•••

During the evening, Burt Brooks goes to the home of his neighbor, Mrs. Mabel Burgard, who lives on a farm a few miles west of Avalon, to talk to her about some livestock.

There is no answer at the house, and it is apparent that the daily chores have not been done.

Brooks looks through a window and sees a body sitting in a rocking chair, covered with a blanket.

Brooks calls in Sheriff W. C. Uhrmacher, and they go into the house to find that it is Mrs. Burgard in the chair with a single bullet wound in her forehead.

Mabel's son Irvin, 15, is nowhere to be found.

Irvin Burgard has been taking care of the family farm since his father died three years ago.

Missing from the farm are a .22 rifle and a 1928 Chevrolet Sedan.

•••

In southwestern Missouri, five McDonald County Deputies are assigned to look out for those who are responsible for a series of robberies and kidnappings spanning from Kansas City to Joplin over the past weekend.

Sergeant Kahler of the State Patrol believes the crimes may have been committed by Texas jail fugitives Floyd Hamilton and Huron Ted Walters.

Deputy Ted Rogers engages in a high-speed chase with a car occupied by two men, and overtakes the vehicle. The men give up without resistance.

At the County Jail in Pinewood, both men will only give their names as "Wilson."

Sheriff Floyd Bone is able to get them to admit to taking part in robberies and kidnappings in the area over the past several days, but they claim not to have committed the robberies in Rich Hill and Harrisonville, nor to the kidnapping of Robert Kalousek.

It is determined that one of the men is Woodrow Elkins, an escaped Oklahoma convict, and that the other is Charles Coates, a fugitive from the Keytesville jail.

August 2, 1938

Tuesday

Woodrow Elkins and Charles Coates escape from the McDonald County jail by picking a lock while they are unguarded.

Elkins is recaptured within several minutes, but Coates steals a car and his whereabouts is unknown.

August 3, 1938

Wednesday

12:10 a.m.

Perry Highley, Rip Robinson, and Walter Glessing, three boys from Farmington, Missouri, are drinking sodas at the refreshment stand at the St. Francois County Recreation Club on Highway 261, four miles north of Farmington, when three men enter the club.

Owners Mr. and Mrs. Vergil Bufford and their daughters are waiting on the customers, including a party of two women and six men in the adjoining room housing the dance floor.

The three men order beers, and while they are being served, Mr. Bufford goes into the next room on an errand. When he returns, one of the men jumps over the bar with a sawed off shotgun. He orders the Buffords to raise their hands, and tells the three Farmington boys to go into the dance hall. The other two men draw pistols and order those in the next room to lie down on the floor.

The man with the shotgun takes a little over $100 from the cash register while the other two search the pockets of the men lying on the dance floor. The women and the three Farmington boys are not searched.

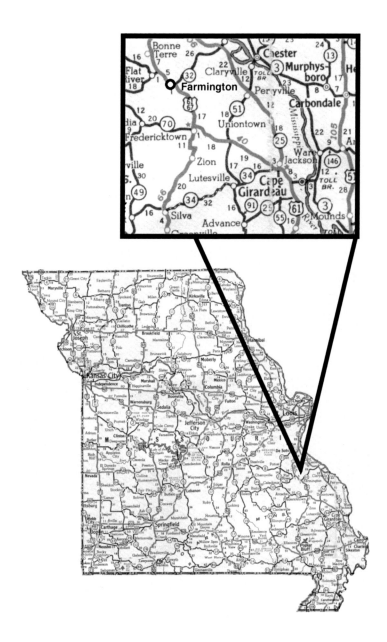

Charles Smith, an electrical foreman on the construction work at the state hospital nearby, hands over his pocketbook and requests that he be allowed to keep his union card and papers. His request is granted. While removing his papers, he is able to slip out a ten dollar bill, but $18 remains for the bandits.

The man next to Smith, who is also involved in construction at the hospital, places his pocketbook containing more than $200 under his stomach and refuses to give it up. One of the men kicks him, and then pistol whips him in the head with the butt of a pistol with such force that the gun is knocked from his hand. He quickly recovers the gun and takes the pocketbook.

The bandits net about $410 in cash. No jewelry is taken.

The bandits order everyone to remain lying on the floor as they back through the main door and make their escape.

•••

3:30 a.m.

Couch, Meredith and Reed drive past two girls sitting on a bridge outside of Cape Girardeau, Missouri.

Reed suggests that they should turn back and pick them up.

They turn the car around and ask the girls if they want a lift. They accept the invitation.

Lorraine Rooney climbs into the back seat with John, and Ruth Baker gets in the front with Jimmy Reed and Jack Meredith.

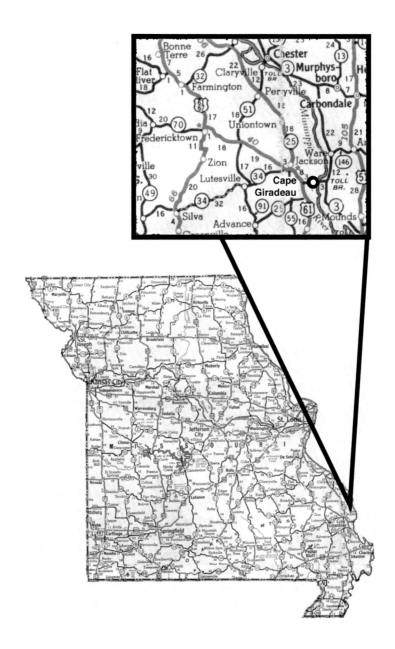

Lorraine Rooney and Ruth Baker
(Not certain who is whom)

Ruth Baker

Bertha Lee "Ruth" Baker was born at Gleason, Tennessee, on December 25, 1916, to Henry and Ida Mae Baker. She attended grade school at Dresden, Tennessee. She married Louis Melton in 1925 (at age 8), and lived with him in Dresden until divorcing him in 1928 (at age 11). She resided in Paducah, Kentucky, from 1928 to 1930. She then moved to St. Louis and married Elmer Taylor, from whom she divorced in 1932. That same year she married Ralph Edwards, from whom she has never obtained a divorce.

She worked as a waitress in various restaurants until 1935, when she began hustling. She has no criminal record, other than some local arrests for prostitution. Her "clinic" name is Peggy Smith.

Ruth is 21 years old, 5' 9", 122 lbs., has brown hair dyed auburn, gray eyes and is of medium complexion.

Baker has multiple tattoos, including a horseshoe with the words "Good Luck," also the letters "WWO" on her right upper arm outer; a rose and the letters "RFD" on her right arm lower outer; the word "ELMER" and the letters "WAH", clasped hands, and "HAROLD MAE" on her left upper arm outer; birds and butterfly left arm outer lower; a dog and the name "JESSE CHAFFIN" on the front of her right thigh; and a kewpie doll with the initials "EEB" and the name "DEB JOHNSON" on the front of her left thigh.

She has known Lorraine Rooney for about six months, from where they hustled around the area of 208 South 6th Street in St. Louis.

•••

Lorraine Rooney

Hattie May Stevens, alias Lorraine Rooney, was born in New Madrid, Missouri, on September 8, 1914, to Sarah and Stephen Stevens.

At age four, Louis Hodge and his wife took Hattie to Bono, Arkansas, where she attended school. She married Everett Hodge, a nephew of Louis Hodge, at age fifteen, and they lived at Kennett, Missouri, until 1930. From 1930 until 1934 they lived at White Oak, Missouri, where Hodge was a bootlegger.

Hattie left Hodge and moved to St. Louis.

Hattie then went to Paragould, Arkansas, where she met Louie Older Bass. They married in July 1937. She lived with Bass in Paragould until March 1938, at which time she went back to St. Louis to hustle, as she had done there before marrying Bass.

Lorraine is 23 years old, 5' 6-3/4", 115 lbs., slender, with dark chestnut hair, blue eyes and of fair complexion.

Rooney has a tattoo of a banner with "SSA 331-14-1333" and the initials "HMSB" in blue and red on her right shoulder; a double short banner with "OLDER" and "HETTIE" and the word "Love" above the initials "LRB" on her right upper arm outer; a Cowboy with "Texas" above and "John" below on the left forearm outer; and a heart with the name "Pat" in it on her right leg, just above the knee.

•••

Rooney wanted to visit her husband, Louie Older Bass, in Paragould, Arkansas. Baker decided to accompany her.

Rooney and Baker left St. Louis about 3:30 p.m. August 2nd, and hitchhiked to Cape Girardeau, Missouri, arriving at the railroad viaduct just before 3:00 a.m. on August 3rd.

Couch asks the girls where they are heading.

Rooney says that she wants to go to Paragould, Arkansas, to visit her husband, and the three men oblige to drive them there.

One of the men said to the women that they might visit relatives in the Texas panhandle, and possibly do a little fishing. Lorraine mentions that she has a sister, Alfene Howell, who lives in Nacogdoches, Texas. The men say they will take them to Paragould, and then on to Texas.

They arrive in Paragould about 7:00 a.m. The girls check into the Cole's Hotel as, "Lorraine and Betty," and are assigned room 8. The men are to meet them there later.

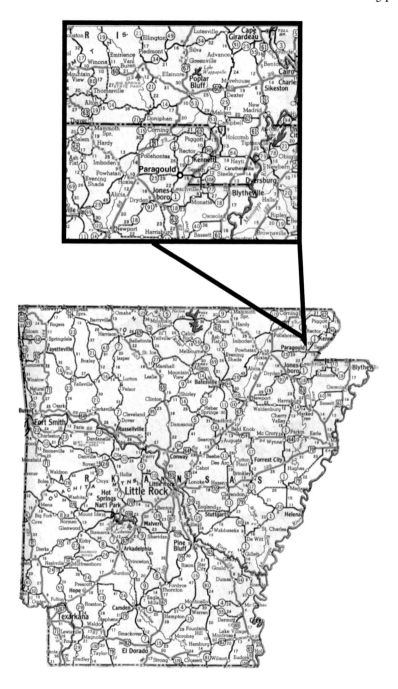

Cole's Hotel
Paragould, Arkansas

Ruth stays at the hotel while Lorraine goes to see her husband. Lorraine returns about 10:00 a.m.

The men rent a room on the same floor, and the group engages in a round of drinking.

In the middle of the afternoon, Jimmy Reed leaves for a while, and returns with Mildred, a "chippy" that he had met downtown.

Jimmy suggests buying a rifle that he saw downtown. He collects $12 each from John and Jack and leaves with Mildred to buy the 30-30 lever action rifle for $36. He returns in about an hour with the rifle and three boxes of shells.

Couch and Meredith take the car to drive around Paragould.

While they are stopped at a stop sign, a policeman pulls up along side them and asks, "Where are you going?" It looks as if he is reaching for a badge or a gun, and Couch tells Meredith to take off, and they lose the officer.

They return to the Cole's Hotel and tell the others that they must leave right away.

Intending to go to Texas by way of Texarkana, Arkansas, they get on the wrong road and end up in back in Missouri. They decide to stay at a combination filling station, tourist camp and dance hall called the "Wakefield Arms," outside of Holcomb, Missouri.

Ruth and Jack stay in one cabin. Lorraine and John in another.

Jimmy takes the car and spends the night elsewhere.

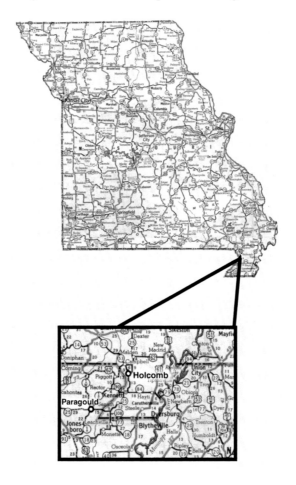

August 4, 1938

Thursday

Jimmy Reed awakes to find that he has been relieved of about $40 and heads back to the tourist camp where the others are staying. He talks them into going with him to get his money back.

The five leave the camp around 9:30 a.m. and proceed to the Eleanor Bullock farm near Holcomb.

Mrs. Bullock and her son Thad are beaten on the head with pistols, and forced to lie on the ground while two of the men go through their clothing looking for money.

As the bandits flee, they fire several shots in the general direction of the Bullocks.

Outside of Blytheville, Arkansas, Jimmy wants to buy more whiskey, but Jack and John protest.

Meredith and Couch tell Reed that they will drop him off at a liquor store, but will leave him there.

Reed replies, "You wouldn't do that."

Couch challenges him to test them.

They stop at a liquor store in Blytheville. Once Reed is inside, they give his hat, coat and $5 to the filling station attendant nearby to give to him when he comes out, and they take off.

When Reed realizes that he has been abandoned, he goes back inside and tries to trade the bottle of whiskey back for money. The proprietor is apprehensive, but returns the money. After Reed leaves, he notifies authorities of a suspicious character.

Couch, Meredith and the girls leave Blytheville, and head south through Arkansas.

They arrive in Arkadelphia about 9:00 p.m., where they stop at a tourist camp on the outskirts of town.

Ruth and Jack take one cabin. Lorraine and John take another.

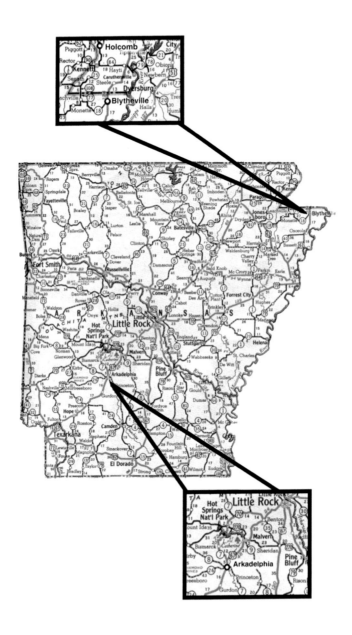

August 5, 1938

Friday

Jimmy Reed spent last night in Blytheville, and is arrested this morning by local authorities. He is placed in the custody of the Sheriff at Kennett, Missouri, on a charge of armed robbery for the Bullock farm incident.

•••

The 1928 Chevrolet Sedan, missing from the home of Mrs. Mabel Burgard who was murdered last Sunday night, is discovered in some brush about a mile and a half from her farm near Avalon, Missouri.

The battery stolen from Jewell Wheeler's car Sunday night has been installed in the vehicle, however, the authorities do not find his missing license plates, or his chauffeur's license.

There is still no sign of 15-year old Irvin Burgard, who is believed to have committed the murder.

•••

From the tourist camp in Arkadelphia, Arkansas, Couch, Meredith and the two girls travel to Texarkana, Arkansas, where they visit Meredith's grandparents, James and Ella Cockrell, who live in an old yellow frame house at 927 Beech Street. Meredith's aunt and uncle, Joseph and Ada Tubbs, are also present while they are visiting. Jack tells his grandparents that he has a friend, his wife and her sister with him.

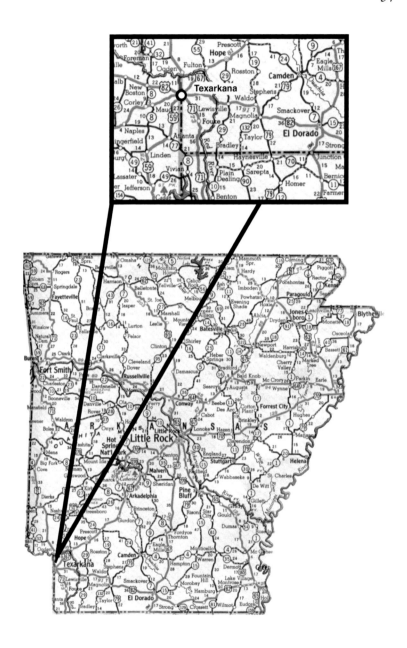

Jack's grandmother asks "Otis" where his car is. He says that none of the other three can drive, so he is driving them on a trip in their car.

Otis agrees to take his grandparents, uncle and aunt to visit another aunt who lives in a small town in Texas, later.

The four visit Otis' relatives for about a half hour, and then head to State Line Tourist Camp, about 36 blocks north from the Texarkana Post Office on State Line Road on the Texas side.

The State Line Camp consists of about ten white cabins with outside showers, located across the street from a cemetery with a steel fence around it.

Jack registers them. They stay in a double cabin.

About 1:00 p.m., Ruth and Jack go back to his grandparents' house, where they pick up his grandmother and his aunt, and they drive to into Texas to visit the other aunt that they call "Red," who lives about twenty miles from Texarkana. They stay for dinner, and then head back to the grandparents' house about 6:00 p.m.

Jack and Ruth get back to the tourist camp about 8:00 p.m.

That evening, Baker and Rooney discover that the men have three pistols and a sawed off double-barrel shotgun in addition to the new rifle which was purchased in Paragould. They assume that the automobile must be stolen and that Couch and Meredith have most likely been involved in some robbery or holdup. They discuss leaving the men, but decide not to do so.

August 6, 1938

Saturday

8:00 a.m.

Couch, Meredith and the two girls leave the tourist camp and head into Texas.

They arrive in Dallas, Texas, around 6:00 p.m.

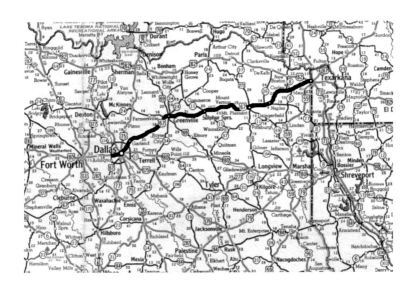

On the west side of Dallas they stop for gas. Couch tells Baker that he is a convict from the Missouri State Penitentiary, and that he has his parole papers with him. He takes the papers out of his pocket and tears them up.

They then stop at a barbeque stand/dancehall on the outskirts of Dallas near Westmoreland and the Dallas-Fort Worth Pike.

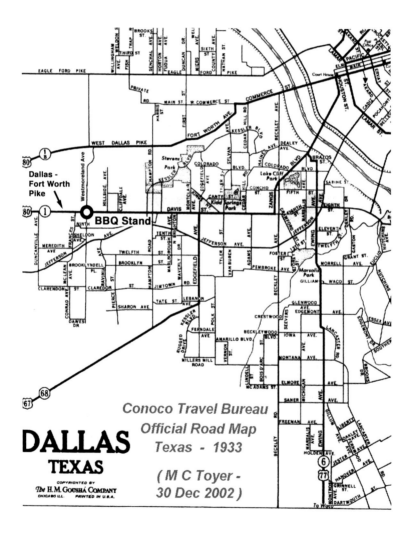

They have ham sandwiches and beer, and the girls go inside to dance, while Couch and Meredith remain outside resting in the car.

They stay at the barbeque stand until around 9:30 p.m. Meredith blows the car horn and Baker and Rooney come back to the car. Baker mentions that there is a patrol car nearby.

Couch looks around and sees the police car behind them. It has a red "STOP" light across the center of it.

Couch and Meredith tell the girls to get into the car, and they speed away.

They get about a half-mile down the road towards Fort Worth, when Dallas City Patrolmen Earl Mowatt and W. E. Lasseter pull up alongside their car. One of the officers yells, "Pull over there, you."

Couch looks up into the rear view mirror, and sees Meredith looking back at him. Couch tells him to, "give her the gas." Meredith hits the accelerator, and the officers flip on their red "STOP" light and siren.

When the officers see that they are getting away, they commence shooting. Their first shot misses, but their second shot hits the car. Jack slumps down in the driver's seat and shoves Baker down in the other front seat. "Get them John," Meredith shouts. "Do not let them get us."

John answers, "I'll do the best I can."

John, who is in the rear seat with Lorraine Rooney, grabs a pistol and starts firing at the officers. He helps Rooney over into the front seat and breaks the glass out of the rear windshield. He continues to shoot at the officers with all of the guns that they have. The girls reload the guns with ammunition.

Numerous shots are exchanged between the bandits and the officers, which results in several automobiles on the highway being struck by stray bullets during the chase.

The officers are gaining on them, so Couch picks up the shotgun and shoots twice at them. He hits the windshield and the front of their car, and Officers Mowatt and Lassiter pull over to the side of the road and park. They telephone ahead to authorities at Arlington.

At Arlington, Police Chief Ott Cribbs hastily gathers a group of patrolmen in his car and starts cruising down the Dallas-Fort Worth Pike.

At Grand Prairie, Chief of Police Perry Nash and Officer W. E. Davis see the Kalousek car speed by them. Thinking that they are just Saturday night joy riders, they pursue them. Couch fires a shotgun blast into their windshield, and the officers hit the ditch.

Cribbs and his men catch up with Couch and Meredith on the west side of Arlington.

Couch continues to fire his shotgun and 30-30 rifle at Cribbs' car, hitting it several times. Cribbs continues pursuit in the damaged car, but Couch and Meredith are able to advance well ahead of them.

On the outskirts of Fort Worth, Meredith turns right off of the main highway into a farmers yard, and they watch as two patrol cars continue right on past them on the highway.

They drive through a closed gate and proceed across a field. After continuing a ways, the car gets bogged down, and they all get out of the car.

John and Jack take the guns, but they leave their clothes in the Kalousek Buick and head off into the woods.

Rooney and Baker go a short way from the vehicle, where they wait a while, then return to the car to get their clothes. They head out across the field and come out to the highway at the same spot that they went in.

The girls walk to a filling station nearby at 1801 Lancaster Street in Fort Worth, and call a taxicab to drive them up and down the Dallas-Fort Worth Pike looking for Couch and Meredith. Not finding them, they go to a tourist camp near Fort Worth, where they spend the rest of Saturday night and part of Sunday. They register as Hattie Bass and Betty Smith.

John and Jack keep a low profile, slowly heading back east through the woods.

August 7, 1938

Sunday

Baker and Rooney register at the A A Tourist Court, 2136 West 7th Street, Fort Worth, under the name of "Jacque Smith and party," of 208 South 6th Street, St. Louis, Missouri.

August 8, 1938

Monday

The girls leave the tourist camp in the morning and go to the depot in Fort Worth to send their suitcase back to St. Louis through the Railway Express Company.

They ship the luggage to Lorraine Rooney, 208 South 6th Street, St. Louis, Missouri.

The girls then start hitchhiking back to St. Louis.

•••

9:30 a.m.

M. C. Smith telephones the Fort Worth Police Department to report a Buick vehicle abandoned around the 2300 block of the Dallas-Fort Worth Pike. The car appears to have been fired into and the glass in the rear doors and the rear window have been broken.

Smith came upon the vehicle while hunting squirrels in the river bottom. He claims that two men with guns came out of the woods and told him to leave.

Smith reports to a newspaper that he had picked out photos of Floyd Hamilton and Huron Ted Walters as the men he saw in the woods. He described them as being around 30 and both bald-headed. Fort Worth police qualify that Smith had been shown only photos of Hamilton and Walters.

The vehicle is investigated and towed to the police station for fingerprinting by V. A. Leonard. It still bears the original Kalousek license plates. The rear windshield and both rear side windows are broken out, and the left rear door has a bullet hole by the handle. Otherwise the car is in fairly good running condition.

Items removed from the car and saved as evidence include:

- Brown wrapping paper with the name A.L. Atkins Dry Goods Co., Rockwell, TX
- A shirt with the name O'NEAL stamped with ink
- A white shirt with the name COUCH stamped in ink
- A brown shirt, a gray shirt, and a brown checked shirt
- A white shirt spattered with blood
- A white handkerchief with the initial "C"
- A white handkerchief with the initial "N"

- A pair of red wool swimming trunks labeled ALLEN A. LIFE GUARD
- Three pair of new gray size 34 trousers (all different makes)
- A pair of blue wool size 32 trousers
- A pair of gray size 32 trousers stamped with O'NEAL C.T.
- A pair of size 32 plaid trousers
- A pair of gray trousers size 28
- A very dirt gray cap, size 7 1/8
- A gray cap labeled GOOD LUCK STORE, ST LOUIS, MO 812 FRANKLIN AVE
- A blue mans wool jacket, and an oxford gray mans coat
- An empty stationery box with the name JACK LANNON written on bottom
- A pair of size 9 roller skates
- A Spanish pistol #01112, .38 caliber, made by Beistegui Brothers (The bullets had to be trimmed to fit this gun)
- A Billy Club made of rubber hose
- A partial box of .32 caliber Western cartridges
- An empty box 30-30 Winchester cartridges
- 2 empty boxes .38 caliber Western Lubaloy cartridges
- A roll 2 1/2" wide white tape
- Several empty 30-30 shells
- Six 12 gauge Remington Shot Shells, #4 shot
- A Barlow Lincoln brand pocketknife
- An Imperial brand pocketknife
- Seven rolls of radio wire
- A business card for Night Hawk Sandwich Systems, 4385 Lee
- A business card for Empire Cleaners, 4119 Evans Ave

•••

A fold containing several personal papers belonging to Meredith is found at Crowley's Ridge State Park in Walcott, Arkansas, (near Paragould) by concessionaire W. R. Heagler.

•••

James A. Davenport, 55, is a truck farmer who raises fruit about one half mile south of Death Crossing in Arlington, Texas.

Davenport is waiting for the bus at Death Crossing shortly after 6:00 p.m., to meet some ladies who are arriving on the bus from Fort Worth. Death Crossing is a three-way intersection with the train tracks of Division, Fielder, and Abraham Streets on the west side of Arlington, where many fatal accidents have occurred.

"I was wiping the windshield of my car when I heard someone call to ask if that was the right road to Dallas," Davenport said. "I told them it was, and then they asked if it was the short cut road to Arlington. I answered that it was and turned my back on them to resume wiping my windshield when they both drew guns on me and said not to make any holler and get back in that car. I said, 'Hey Fellows, what is the matter with you anyway?' I had a peculiar sensation when I turned my back on them the first time."

Davenport gets into the back seat of his car with Couch, while Jack takes the wheel and heads for Dallas. They have Davenport direct them through Arlington over a circuitous route so that the car will not be recognized on the Fort Worth-Dallas Pike.

Davenport is forced to lie down in the car, but near Grand Prairie he is allowed to get up, with the orders that he will be shot if he attracts attention in any way.

After reaching Dallas, they drive on Highway 67, which heads northeast back towards Texarkana.

"While I was lying down between the front and back seats with a pistol pressed against my head," Davenport related, "I told them I understood perfectly the whole thing and had sense enough to do what they told me. One of them said, 'I hate to do this to you Dad, but it is a life and death case with us. Don't you get us into a jam and tell us right where we are going.'"

"Then I explained to them who I was in answer to their questions. They asked why I was at the bus station, why were people coming in on the bus, where I lived and who with and what people would think when I failed to meet them or did not come back that night."

"At Grand Prairie, and all other towns, they were very careful to observe every traffic rule and were more careful than the ordinary driver. There was no cussing, no drinking and they were surprisingly nice to me. I told them I was not scared nor nervous, and did not want them to be nervous or get me into a jam. I explained that all three of us were already in a jam and that I wanted to save my life and my car, if the latter was possible. I sold them on the fact I would not give them away, thereby gaining their confidence on such forced short acquaintance."

"They asked me if I wanted to know the truth about their trouble that started at Dallas. I said I did. They said they had a car and two girls. The girls had over $500 so they all decided to go to south Texas fishing. On Highway 4 near Dallas they drove up to a drinking place where the girls wanted to dance. The men told them they were too tired and dirty, but for them to go in and dance. They did so, but kept coming back to the car to talk. They told them to quit that as it would cause suspicion that the place would be robbed after the girls had furnished the information on the layout. They got in the car and were all sitting there when the officers came up and began questioning them.

They couldn't stand being frisked because they had guns, so they decided to try to get away. The officers fired the first shot as they tore out."

"They sure liked to have piled up in a big wreck in Arlington. At a traffic light, which they ran on red, the cars were so thick they couldn't see any way through but they sat down on the horn and a lane opened up just barely big enough to get through. They sure got lucky there. They said the girls later got shot up and were in a hospital but did not say where."

Couch and Meredith boast that they will round up a gang of six and come back to this section to "mop up."

Davenport talked fast during every lag in conversation because he did not want to discuss shooting.

"They promised to leave me in Dallas, before we got there, and leave the car there that night. I was nervous in Dallas, afraid officers would recognize us and start shooting. They asked me how to get out of Dallas and I knew they knew the roads out. I told them I did not know the roads out. They bragged on my car and its good lights. We went through Greenville. They parked in a loading zone, but backed out and reparked when they discovered it. They asked if I was hungry. I told them no, I had no appetite but would like a Coca-Cola. They called a Mexican and bought tamales and cold drinks. We stayed there in plain view 20 minutes, but saw no officers. They questioned me about the gas gauge and how far the car would go before needing gas. They put in 12 gallons, which settled that question for some time. They stopped at another filling station and I thought they were going to hijack it, but they bought cigarettes as they were out after smoking up mine."

"They kept telling me they were going to let me out, but we went through town after town without that happening. Finally they said they were going to do me a favor by letting me out. Said they were going to take my clothing and money.

'That's sure sweet of you,' I answered, and meant it."

"'What will you do?' they asked. 'I will phone home for money,' I replied, 'and you would do the same.' They took my purse, emptied it and handed it back." Davenport had about $4 on him at the time.

"The one named Jack apologized to me fifty times. Said it was a mean thing they were doing to an old man. I asked them to leave me one dollar, but they refused. Then they again said they were going to let me out. 'Fine,' I replied, 'for I am getting tired.' They were surprised at my being tired, when I explained to them that I was not accustomed to that kind of thing but they probably were, and reminded them I was going through a great mental strain."

Couch and Meredith tell Davenport that he is the coolest man they've ever held up.

Both of the bandits are in shirtsleeves. Jack wears a greenish felt hat.

John explains to Davenport that he had been hit on the head by a guard while in some institution, which has dented his skull right in the center of the top off his head. A silver plate had to be inserted in his skull.

"Then they gave me the choice of being tied up or undressing, and I told them it would be cruel to tie me up. The boy in front wanted me to have my shoes but the other one wanted to wear them, as they were his size. They said they would drop my clothes a half mile up the road and I could get them."

"They asked me what time it was. I looked at my watch and they questioned me as to its value. I explained that it was a gift and not worth more than $1 to them for pawning, stating I knew they had more sense than to risk being caught for $1. They let me keep my watch. They told me to undress and asked about my cigarette supply and matches, one giving me four and the other two matches."

Approximately a mile west of Bassett, Texas, the fugitives stop the car and order Davenport out, clothed only in underwear and socks, saying they need his car for a trip, but not divulging where.

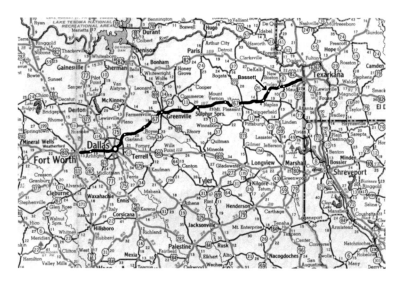

"As they let me out I thought probably they would shoot me so I took my time getting out. They shook my hand telling me goodnight. I told them to keep out of a jam and let me recover my car. They said they would, unless they got into a fight with officers, where the car probably would be wrecked. They kept shaking my hand like we were old friends and telling me goodnight, so it took them a long time to go. As they left they said they would send me $100 later."

"I have been in every state in the Union, and know most all the scenic spots of beauty in this country, but when I was out of gun shot and saw my own car being taken by the bandits, it was the most beautiful sight I ever saw. You can't imagine the relief I felt. I just sat down until they got around the curve and out of sight. Then I went down the road trying to find my clothes. Over a small bridge I saw what I believed was a bundle, but after creeping over stones, weeds and dewy grass with tender feet, I only found an old paper. Cars passed and hollered to me but did not stop. One finally stopped, and I told them I was in trouble and needed help, but they just drove off. Walking into Bassett, I got a lady to listen to my story. Mr. W. J. Johnston, Postmaster of Bassett and grocery man of Johnston's Country Store, opened his store, listened to my story and let me in to phone Arlington what had happened to me."

Bassett is about 35 miles southwest of Texarkana, Texas.

Davenport had been instructed by Couch and Meredith to not call police, which he does not. Johnston, however, does notify the Texarkana, Texas, police about the incident at 11:45 p.m.

After relatives became alarmed at Davenport's failure to return home, Arlington and Fort Worth police were notified. About an hour after Davenport's call came through, several of his family members came for him.

Davenport is shown photos of Hamilton and Walters, but he states positively that there is no resemblance between them and the two men who had robbed him.

Couch and Meredith drive the Davenport Car several miles down the road from where they dropped Davenport off when the car suddenly stalls. They abandon the vehicle and take refuge in the woods.

[AUTHOR'S NOTE: Although I have come across no examples of it in researching this book, I hope that some newspaper somewhere took advantage of the headline: COUCH KIDNAPS DAVENPORT!]

August 9, 1938

Tuesday

   Couch and Meredith lay low in the woods for a while, then head to the train tracks to start their journey back to St. Louis.

•••

   Ruth Baker and Lorraine Rooney arrive back in St. Louis about 5:00 p.m.
   During their travels, Baker had given John and Jack her address as 208 South 6th Street in St. Louis, and her phone number, GARfield 6348.
   Though no formal arrangements had been made, the women think there is a possibility that the men may try and meet them in St. Louis.

August 10, 1938

Wednesday

   Lorraine Rooney and Ruth Baker are arrested by the FBI in a rooming house in the 200 block of South Sixth Street in St. Louis.
   The FBI Agents who apprehended them say they were traced through clothing expressed to the St. Louis address from Dallas, Texas. They made the arrests after waiting futilely in hope their companions might rejoin them.
   They give their names as Ruby Baker (alias Peggy Smith), 22, from Gleason, Tennessee; and Hattie Mae Bass (maiden name Hattie Mae Stevens), 24, from New Madrid, Missouri.

For whatever reason, Baker tells the FBI that they are expecting a call round 11:00 p.m. that evening to meet Couch and Meredith in St. Louis.

August 11, 1938

Thursday

The FBI Office in St. Louis receives a Teletype from the Dallas Office advising that James Clyde Reed, who recently rode with Couch and Meredith, is presently in custody of the Sheriff at Kennett, Missouri, and suggests that the St. Louis Office arrange an immediate interview.

James Clyde Reed, charged with the armed robbery of Eleanor Bullock near Holcomb, Missouri, has told the Sheriff at Kennett that he rode with Couch and Meredith before being arrested in Blytheville, Arkansas. He also says that Couch and Meredith committed two armed robberies and planned to rob a bank.

•••

A complaint is filed before John Davis, US Commissioner for the Northern District of Texas at Dallas, charging John Couch, Otis James Meredieth, Hattie Mae Bass, and Ruby Baker with transporting a stolen vehicle across a state line.

•••

Floyd Hamilton and Huron Ted Walters are hunted in the east Texas oil field area.

A woman who said that she knew both Floyd Hamilton and his brother Raymond, identified Floyd as one of two men who stopped at a sandwich stand three miles south of Tyler, Texas, yesterday.

Her description of the second man fit that of Huron Ted Walters.

The two men were traveling in an automobile carrying Louisiana license plates.

The men stopped at the stand and ordered food but left before they were served.

Meanwhile, federal agents joined officers of Texas, Louisiana and Arkansas in the hunt for Hamilton and Walters.

The fugitives were charged with transporting a stolen automobile across a state line.

August 12, 1938

Friday

J. B. Foster, of the St. Louis FBI Office, interviews James Clyde Reed at Kennett, Missouri. Reed will not make any statement in writing, but agrees to discuss his association with Couch and Meredith. He adds, however, that he will not hesitate to lie about any pertinent facts that will better serve his purpose.

Reed says that he resides at 4119 Evans Street in St. Louis. He became acquainted with Couch and Meredith while they were incarcerated at the Missouri State Penitentiary in Jefferson City, Missouri. He is presently on parole from Jefferson City, having been sentenced in December 1930 to ten years on a robbery charge. He was paroled in January 1937. During July 1938 he met up again with Couch and Meredith. He claims Couch and Meredith came to his house on August 2nd, accompanied by two women, at which time Couch and Meredith told Reed that they were planning on robbing a bank somewhere around Memphis, Tennessee, and they wanted Reed to go with them. He says that he packed his clothes and went with them and they traveled south. About 100 miles out of St. Louis, Couch and Meredith advise Reed that the

Buick in which they are riding is "hot," being stolen from around Kansas City, to which Reed replied, "Isn't that too bad."

He tells of going to Paragould and purchasing the rifle. He said Couch and Meredith returned to the Cole's Hotel where they were staying, and said they had to get out right away, and proceeded to a tourist camp called the Wakefield Arms near Holcomb, Missouri. There, Couch and Meredith allowed him to use the car to scout for a woman for himself. He says he found a prostitute, with whom he spent the night at another tourist camp near the Wakefield Arms. In the morning he realizes that he had been rolled and went back to the Wakefield Arms to get Couch and Meredith to go with him to find the prostitute and get his money returned. He stated he had a fight with this prostitute on this occasion, and he believes that this is the charge of armed robbery on which he is being held.

Reed says that Couch and Meredith abandoned him in Blytheville, Arkansas, on August 4th, when he went into a tavern to get a sandwich and some more liquor. He spent the night in Blytheville and was arrested on the morning of August 5th. Reed positively denies being with Couch and Meredith at Greenwood, Missouri, when Robert Kalousek was kidnapped and his car stolen.

•••

Floyd Hamilton and Huron Ted Walters hold up the Coca-Cola Bottling Company at 117 West Hempstead in Nashville, Arkansas. Pulling handkerchiefs over their faces, they walk in to the office where Manager Forrest Wilson is talking with City Water Superintendent, Hugh B. Caruthers.

Upon entering, Hamilton says, "We want your money. We mean business."

They have Wilson open the safe and give the cash drawer containing currency, change and checks to Hamilton.

As the bandits are leaving, Wilson says, "You won't need those checks."

Hamilton snaps back, "All right," and puts the cash drawer on the desk. With a gun in one hand, he sorts out the checks, lays them to one side, picks up the cash drawer and leaves the same way he had entered.

The pair made off with $67.36.

They are able to break through one police barricade set up for them, before their car is disabled from police gunfire from a second barricade. They commandeer a vehicle that is approaching behind them and drive into the woods, avoiding capture.

•••

Couch and Meredith make their way back to St. Louis on a freight train.

At the freight yard in St. Louis they are spotted by a railroad officer, but they manage to escape him.

They seek refuge with John's sister, Frances Whitter, who lives at 3709 Cass Avenue. She informs them that they are already being sought by authorities and she cannot permit them to stay in her house.

Couch and Meredith take off, walking the streets through the evening trying to come up with their next plan of action.

August 13, 1938

Saturday

12:30 a.m.

Daniel Cox Fahey, Jr. and Peggy Gross are parked on Warson Road, about a block from Peggy's home at 10 Picardy Lane in Clayton, an inner ring suburb of St. Louis.

Peggy Gross   **Daniel Cox Fahey, Jr.**

Miss Gross, 23, is a member of the younger social set, and her family is prominent in St. Louis society. She is 5' 6-1/2", 110 lbs., with light brown hair, hazel eyes and of slender build.

Fahey, 31, came to St. Louis about three years ago from Washington, D.C. He has been contracted with drafting plans for the St. Louis Jefferson Memorial Riverfront Improvement

Project. He is 6' 1" tall, 180 lbs., brown hair, blue eyes, and of slender build.

They have just returned from an outdoor "Little Symphony" concert at Shaw Park in Clayton.

Two men approach from the rear of the car and announce, "This is a holdup."

Fahey hits the starter on his car, but one of the men jumps on the running board and hits him on the nose with the butt end of a revolver. Fahey's nose bleeds freely, but he remains conscious. The two men place Fahey and Miss Gross into the back of the car and they get into the front.

They drive north on Warson Road, then head west on Olive Street. They then take the No. 40 cutoff, when one of the men asks Fahey how much gas is in the car.

"Not very much," he replies, knowing actually that they have half a tank and that the gas gauge does not work.

They drive down the cutoff about two miles and then turn south down a side road about 100 yards with the lights off and stop. John gets out of the car with Fahey and Miss Gross. He keeps a gun on the two and makes them sit on the ground. It is a bright moonlit night.

Jack drives the car out to the No. 40 cutoff and drives to a filling station about a half mile east of the dirt road. He buys gas and some Lucky Strikes, and then goes back to pick up the other three.

They head back to the main road again and turn west, continuing over the new bridge over the Missouri River to Wentzville, Missouri, where the No. 40 cutoff joins US 40 and intersects with US 61.

They head north on US 61.

John asks Fahey how much money he has.

Fahey says, "Here's my pocketbook, just take it."

John asks, "Do you have a watch?"

Fahey replies, "No," even though he does have one in his pocket.

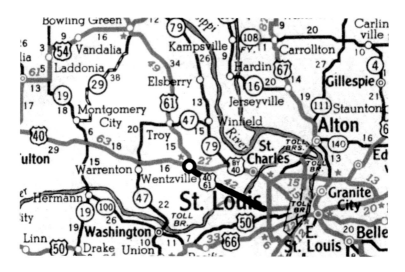

John takes cash out of the pocketbook, which contained about $7. Fahey asks for the pocketbook back since it has his driver's license and papers in it, to which John obliges.

Later, they stop again for gas, with John staying with the couple off of the main road while Jack goes to the station to refuel.

Couch and Meredith say that they have, "a date in Minneapolis at 11 o'clock, we're going to pull a job in North Minneapolis."

They stop again for gas about five miles south of Hannibal, Missouri. This time the captives are allowed to stay in the car, if they promise to behave while at the station.

Later, back on the road, Fahey takes his watch out of his pocket and puts it in Miss Gross' pocketbook.

They continue north on US 61 and it begins to become daylight while they are still in Missouri.

John sees a hardware store on the west side of the road after they pass into Iowa, just south of Keokuk, and mentions that they should get some cartridges for their guns. Jack goes into the store and buys the ammunition.

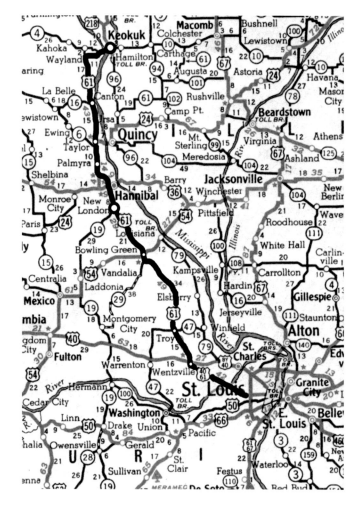

Back on the road, they test the ammunition by shooting at road signs.

9:00 a.m.

They stop somewhere in Iowa for gas. One of the men goes to a café next to the filling station and brings food out to the car. A roast beef or pork sandwich for Miss Gross, a lettuce and tomato sandwich for Fahey, and a bottle of milk for them to share.

The men tell the couple that they intend them no harm, but need their vehicle for transportation, and that they have to take them along to keep them from reporting that the car had been stolen.

During the trip the men talk to each other in low tones and converse with their captives quite often.

Jack tells Peggy and Dan about how they always tie people up when robbing them. He relates tying two individuals in St. Louis for a period of two hours and then going back later to release them.

The men also talk about picking up two old men and threatening to shoot them, whereupon one of the individuals remarked that, "It would be alright with us." They then let the men go.

John is very surly and the most talkative of the two.

John makes remarks about how badly officers had treated his sister when his brother was sent up for killing a policeman in St. Louis. Someone else had admitted to killing the officer, but they charged John's brother anyway. John remarks that he is going back to St. Louis to "fix" the police department.

The men start talking about a place in Minneapolis where they are going to meet "Jim."

They stop occasionally throughout the day for Coca Colas.

John and Jack brag about their exploits. They seem quite proud that the FBI knows about them and that there is a $500 reward out for each of them. They state that they each had been in prison. John says that he had just been paroled June 18th out of Jefferson City to the parole officer in St. Louis.

They say that they had, "celebrated their Fourth of July," a few weeks earlier in a gun battle with officers in Texas, and that they had recently been in Arkansas,

Louisiana, Tennessee and Texas. They say they had picked up two girl hitchhikers, and that these girls were with them during the gun battle in Texas, and that they were separated from them when they abandoned the car near Fort Worth.

They continue north on Highway 61. Fahey and Gross catch naps in the car. They pass though Davenport, Iowa. Jack pulls the car over and they all get out to stretch. Fahey and Miss Gross start to walk away from the car. The men call for them to come back. Fahey suggests to Miss Gross that they should make a dash for it, but she does not do so.

Several cars pass by, but pay no attention to them. Fahey waves his hat at one car. Jack and John order Fahey back and threaten to shoot him if he doesn't obey. John fires off a shot and Fahey starts back to the car. John tries to hit him several times with the butt of his gun, but Fahey dodges every attempt. John puts his gun in Fahey's back. Peggy is frightened and urges Dan to get back into the car.

They continue north on Highway 61.

John reveals at this time that his full name is John Couch.

Just before noon, they enter Dubuque, Iowa. The men tell Fahey, "If you won't try to attract attention, we give you our word to release you and Miss Gross after dark."

They approach a toll bridge high over the Mississippi River into Wisconsin. Fahey tries to make the toll man aware of the blood on his shirt, but nothing is said even though the toll man noticed him. Jack pays the toll and continues on.

A half-mile past the bridge, they fill up with gas at a filling station on the east side of the road. Jack pulls a wad of bills out of his pocket and pays for the gas.

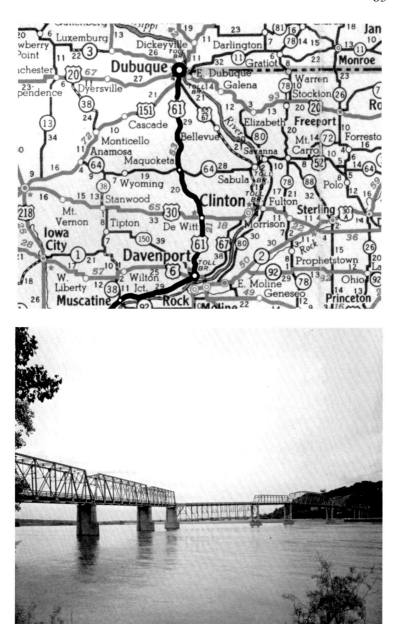

Eagle Point Bridge
Dubuque, Iowa

They continue north on Highway 61, where they pass a Catholic Church in Dickeyville, Wisconsin. There is a large stone grotto along the side of the road and Jack turns the car around to have a closer look. He is quite interested in it.

Shortly after noon, they stop in a town in Wisconsin for lunch. Peggy has a hamburger, Dan has a lettuce and tomato sandwich, and they share a pint of milk. They eat the meal in the car.

Midafternoon they stop again for gas and to air up the tires. While John takes care of the car, Jack and Peggy go into a soft drink stand nearby. Peggy comes back to the car about ten minutes later and says that Jack has asked her to write to his mother, but he has not given her the address.

Jack has given Peggy a newspaper clipping about James Clyde Reed, who was being interviewed by officers in Missouri.

EX-CONVICT GRILLED IN SERIES OF HOLD-UPS

By Associated Press

Jefferson City, Mo., August 6

Colonel B. Marvin Casteel, Superintendent of the State Highway Patrol, today said James Clyde Reed, 26, an ex-convict, held at Kennett, Mo. Is being questioned in connection with a series of robberies and a kidnaping in Western Missouri last Saturday.

Reed denied taking part in the robberies near Kansas City and in the kidnaping of Robert Kalousek at Greenwood, Casteel said. However, Sgt. R. R. Reed of the Highway Patrol, who questioned the suspect, said Reed told him two companions who deserted him at Blytheville, Ark., were involved in the crimes.

Reed, who served a term in the state prison here for robbery in St. Louis in 1930, was quoted by Casteel as saying he and his two companions were on their way to hold up a bank when his companions picked up two girls and abandoned him.

Reed was arrested in St. Louis December 14, 1930, in the 4200 block of Delmar Boulevard after police had pursued him and two companions several blocks. After his arrest he confessed to holding up a drug store a few minutes previous. He also confessed to holding up a dry goods store prior to his arrest.

In March 1931 Reed was found guilty of two charges of robbery, and was sentenced to 10 years in the Missouri State Penitentiary. The sentence was commuted to 10 years in the State Reformatory. On June 24 he was transferred to the Penitentiary, from which he was given a conditional commutation by Governor Stark on January 18, 1937.

••••

Two gunmen, one identified as Floyd Hamilton, are the objects of a manhunt in a wooded mountain area along the Arkansas-Oklahoma border, 12 miles north of DeQueen, Arkansas.

The men fled into the woods on foot this afternoon after exchanging shots with Assistant Superintendent Cliff Atkinson of the Arkansas State Police and Deputy Sheriff Leslie Dillahunty of DeQueen. Lieut. Earl Scroggin of the State Police said there was no doubt one of the men was Hamilton.

He said Hamilton's fingerprints were found on articles left in the automobile that the two fugitives had abandoned near Wilton, Arkansas, following the exchange of shots with officers late yesterday.

The other man was believed to be Huron Ted Walters, Hamilton's companion in the holdup of the Bank of Bradley, Arkansas, last June.

Hamilton and Walters are also suspected of committing a $34,000 payroll holdup at Wood River, Illinois, on August 5th.

Atkinson and Dillahunty encountered the fugitives at Ladd's Bridge and fired on them with a machine gun, forcing them to abandon a stolen automobile. The car was riddled with bullets. In it were found two sawed off shotguns, a rifle and an automatic pistol with about 30 rounds of ammunition. Officers expressed belief that the men are still heavily armed.

Bloodhounds brought here from Ashdown, Arkansas, by Sheriff Jim Sanderson were unable to pick up the trail. Sheriff's officers from Daingerfield, Texas, also brought a pack of hounds here, but officers decided not to release them until daylight.

Nearly 40 officers from Arkansas, Oklahoma, and Texas are engaged in searching the woods and patrolling highways tonight.

•••

4:00 p.m.

Couch, Meredith, Gross and Fahey pass through La Crosse, Wisconsin, where they cross the Mississippi river into Minnesota, heading for the Twin Cities, still traveling on Highway 61.

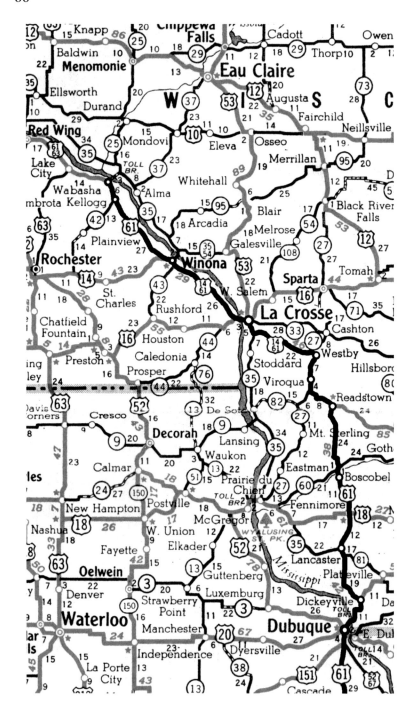

The temperature has reached into the low 90s.

At some town along the way that has a flourmill and an elevator on main street, possibly Wabasha, they stop for supper. Jack goes into a café to order sandwiches. Fahey and Miss Gross are sitting in the back seat of the car. John asks Peggy if she wants to go into the café to use the rest room. Peggy goes into the café across the street from the flourmill and then comes out to use the rest room at the adjoining service station.

After Jack and Peggy return to the car, they eat a supper of hamburgers, peanuts, candy and milk.

They pass through Red Wing, and then into Hastings, where they again cross the Mississippi River on a bridge with a spiral approach.

Spiral Bridge
Hastings, Minnesota

Between Hastings and St. Paul, it is evident that Jack and John are killing time. One of them says that they do not want to get into the Twin Cities until after dark. They drive through St. Paul without stopping, past the University of Minnesota, then across the Mississippi River on Hennepin Avenue into Minneapolis.

90

They turn back east on Lake Street. They pass Lyndale, Nicollet and Portland Avenues before heading north on Cedar, to connect with Washington Avenue.

Dan asks the men when they plan on letting them go. They reply, "Soon."

At about 40th Avenue North and Washington Avenue, they stop the car. Jack turns to the back seat and says, "I'll tell you our proposition. We have a job to pull here in Minneapolis tonight. I'll either let you two go along with us, or we'll take you someplace and tie you up."

Dan and Peggy both agree that they would rather be tied up, to which Jack replies, "All right."

They drive north of Minneapolis on Highway 169, known along this stretch as the West River Road because it parallels the Mississippi River, to a point about 1-1/2 miles south of Champlin.

10:00 p.m.

They find a pasture next to the road, and decide this is a good place to release Dan and Peggy.

They have traveled over 650 mile miles in the last 21-1/2 hours.

They park the car and turn the off lights. A couple of vehicles pass by, but they pay no notice.

All four exit the car. Dan gets a pair of pliers out of the toolkit in his car. Couch and Meredith have some wire that they picked up in a hardware store in southeastern Minnesota.

Dan helps Peggy through the bushes and over a barbwire fence. John tells Dan to lie down on his stomach, and they tie his ankles with wire. Then they tie his wrists behind his back, palms outward. They put a handkerchief in his mouth to gag him. They lay out some Kleenex on the ground so that Dan does not have to lie with his face in the dirt.

John goes to tie up Peggy, who is about 50 feet away from Fahey. John binds Peggy up in a similar fashion to Dan, but he does not gag her. John intimates to Peggy that he could have immoral plans for her, and she cries out for Jack. Meredith threatens to shoot John if he attempts to mishandle Miss Gross.

After the tension eases, Jack remarks that Jim would be mad if they hadn't brought an attractive girl along.

10:30 p.m.

Jack and John bid their victims farewell, saying they needed to meet Jim at 11:00 p.m. in Minneapolis. They comment to Dan that it was a good thing Jim wasn't with them when Fahey tried to attract attention in Iowa, because, "Jim would have shot you."

John and Jack say that after they pull the job with Jim, that they will come back to release them.

Peggy suggests that they not bring Jim back with them.

Jack says that they will just leave Dan's car in North Minneapolis then.

Couch and Meredith wish the pair, "Good luck," to which they respond, "Good luck to you, too."

Newspaper Illustration

Jack tells Peggy, "When you see the Police, tell them not to shoot me in the head. Tell them I'm the nice one."

As soon as they leave, Dan is able to get the handkerchief out of his mouth. He calls to Peggy, who acknowledges that she is all right. He tries to loosen his wrists and ankles, but is unable to do so. He manages to get up on his feet and hobble over to Peggy. They try to untie each other, but have a difficult time with the stiff wire.

Dan hops over to the barbed wire fence near the highway, but is unable to get over it. He tries to hail a couple of vehicles that pass by, but to no avail. A third car travels past him a couple of hundred feet and then turns back. It is Carl Gustafson, a farmer who lives nearby, and his neighbor Roland Reilly, who works for the phone company.

"Please untie me," Fahey pleads, "I'm all bound with wire. I was kidnapped in St. Louis."

"What are you doing, kidding me?" queries Gustafson.

"No, it's true, really," Fahey replies.

Gustafson works for some time loosening Fahey's hands from the wire. Fahey asks him to go back into the woods and look for Miss Gross while he releases his feet.

"I found Miss Gross about 200 feet back in the woods," Gustafson said. "She was lying on the ground and had been bitten badly by mosquitoes. I removed the wire that bound her. She was pretty shaky, but recovered quickly."

Gustafson drives the two to his home, which is about two miles south of Champlin, arriving around 11:00 p.m.

Carl places a call to the Sheriff's Office in Minneapolis. The Sheriff's Deputies arrive to meet them around 11:30 p.m.

Back in St. Louis, Attorney Carl Otto called the St.
Louis FBI Special Agent in Charge, G. B. Norris, at his home.
Otto stated that he was calling on behalf of Mr. Robert
H. Gross, whose 23 year old daughter, Viola Cecilia "Peggy"
Gross, had gone to a Little Symphony Concert at Clayton,
Missouri, with Mr. Daniel Cox Fahey, Jr. the evening before
and she had not been seen since. He stated that Robert Gross is
of excellent reputation, and that although Miss Gross has only
known Fahey about a week, he has lived in St. Louis for two
years and is said to come from a good family.

FBI Agents from the St. Louis office interviewed Mr.
Gross at his house at #10 Picardy Lane in Clayton, a home
previously owned by Missouri Senator Bennett Champ Clark.
Gross advised them that he represented several textile
manufacturing companies, and that his office was at 503 North
12th Street in St. Louis, in the Silk Exchange Building.

He told them that his daughter Peggy left home shortly
after 6:00 p.m. the evening before with Daniel Cox Fahey, Jr.
They had a dinner engagement and planned to attend the Little
Symphony concert at Clayton, Missouri. They had not
returned, and he had not received any information on their
whereabouts. Mr. Gross knows very little about Fahey, except
that he is employed as a landscape architect for the National
Park Service, and has an office in the Old Post Office building
at 8th and Olive Street in St. Louis. He added that Fahey
resides at the home of Samuel Fordyce, at 19 Washington
Terrace. Fordyce is a prominent attorney in St. Louis.

Mr. Gross noted that William Drew, of 470 Lake
Avenue, had observed Peggy and Dan attending the Little
Symphony Concert the previous evening. He also added

that Charles Peterson, who works with Fahey and had dinner with Fahey and Miss Gross the previous evening, told him that Fahey did not report to work on Saturday morning.

None of Fahey's clothing had been removed from his home.

Mr. Gross stated that based on information from Fahey's associates, he does not indulge in intoxicants, and is of excellent character and reputation.

Mr. Gross went on to state that Peggy is engaged to Sewell Pangman, who is currently in Douglas, Michigan. Mr. Gross did not believe that Peggy and Mr. Fahey had eloped, as she was ill recently and had been confined in a St. Louis hospital.

Peggy has no particular hobbies, but plays tennis and swims.

Gross admitted that his daughter does indulge in intoxicants, and on occasions stays out very late, but that she would always advise her family as to her whereabouts. He pointed out that Peggy likes to frequent Culpepper's Bar at Maryland and Euclid and the Canoe Club at Valley Park.

Mr. Gross said that he had already notified the Sheriff's department at Clayton, Missouri, who broadcast the disappearance of Fahey and, "an unknown woman."

Mr. Gross added that Peggy has a brother, John, living at 21 Lincoln Park in Chicago.

Inquiry was made at Culpepper's Tavern, and it was ascertained that Fahey and Miss Gross had not been there the night before.

Agents also interviewed acquaintances of the missing pair.

William Drew knew both Fahey and Gross, and saw them at the concert during the intermission, but did not engage in conversation with them.

Charles Peterson, a landscape architect associate of Fahey, had dinner with Peggy and Dan the evening of August 12th at the home of Samuel Fordyce. During the dinner, Fahey asked Miss Gross if she would like to attend the Little Symphony Concert with him. Both Fahey and Miss Gross invited Mr. Peterson to come along, but he declined and left for his home about 9:05 p.m.

•••

Just before midnight Fahey and Miss Gross are taken to the Hennepin County Sheriff's Office in Minneapolis by Deputy Sheriffs Frank Archambo and Mike Fahey (no relation to Daniel). Gross and Fahey make a brief statement regarding the description of Fahey's car, and a partial description of the subjects.

Fahey tells the deputies that one of the men was called Jack and the other John. Jack weighed about 145 lbs., had dark long hair which was parted in the middle, was dark complexioned, and had tattoo marks on both forearms. He says John weighed about 140 lbs., was dark complexioned and had dark short clipped hair. Jack was about 26 years of age and John was about 24.

This information is put on the radio by the St. Paul and Minneapolis Police Departments in an effort to locate the automobile and apprehend the subjects.

August 14, 1938

Sunday

12:30 a.m.

     Robert Gross notified the St. Louis FBI office that his daughter had called him from the Sheriff's Office in Minneapolis. Gross received several calls from Viola, and in one she claimed she was being held in the Sheriff's Office because of the fact that they suspected the kidnapping story was untrue.

     Mr. Gross also called the St. Paul FBI Office to inquire, and they assured him that Peggy was not in custody, but was being detained for further information.

Nicollet Hotel
Minneapolis, Minnesota

3:00 a.m.

Special Agents A. G. Berens and E. N. Notesteen go to the Nicollet Hotel, at Washington and Hennepin in Minneapolis, where Fahey and Miss Gross obtained rooms after leaving the Hennepin County Sheriff's Office. The room clerk discloses that Fahey is in room 748, and Miss Gross in 746.

The agents head to the 7th floor via the back elevator, assisted by the House Detective. Entering the elevator, they notice a gray shirt and gray trousers hanging on the south wall of the elevator. The House Detective explains that they belong to Fahey. They had bloodstains and were to be cleaned later. The agents advise him to retain the clothing in its present state.

The federal agents, joined by Minneapolis Police Detective Van Rickley, question Fahey in his room for a short period of time. He relates to them in some detail the facts surrounding his abduction. Fahey made mental notes about all the places that they had passed through. He recalls that one of the subjects had told him his full name, or that he heard the full name during conversation with the subjects, but cannot remember it.

They place a call to Miss Gross' room and request to come and talk to her. Agents Berens, Notesteen and S. W. Hardy, who is the Special Agent in Charge of the St. Paul Office in the absence of SAC Robert Hendon, interview Peggy in her room around 3:30 a.m.

Miss Gross corroborates the information given by Fahey. She was sleeping when they called her, and she is quite nervous. The agents decide she should get some rest, and arrangements are made to have Agent Berens call on Gross and Fahey at 10:00 a.m. at the Hotel.

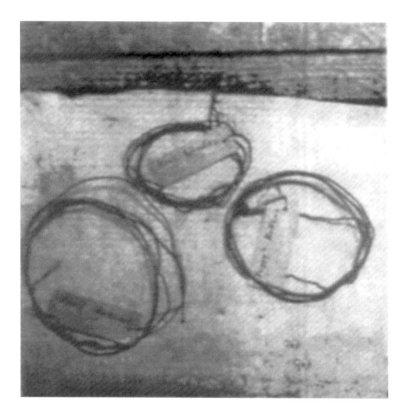

In the morning, Carl Gustafson, who found Fahey and Miss Gross along side the road the evening before, goes back to the scene and finds the pieces of wire used to bind the victims. He tags each wire with a note to the best of his recollection, "wire from Dan's ankles," "wire from Dan's wrists," "wire from Miss Gross' ankles." The wire from Miss Gross' wrists cannot be found. Gustafson turns these over to Agent Notesteen to be retained in the St. Paul Office.

•••

10:00 a.m.

Agent Berens calls upon Peggy Gross and Dan Fahey at the Nicollet Hotel. After having breakfast in Fahey's room, they accompany Berens to the St. Paul FBI Office for further questioning.

The FBI Office is located in the New York Life Building at Sixth and Minnesota in St. Paul. This is an elegant 1890 office building with a large bronze eagle positioned over the entrance.

New York Life Building

Fahey is calm and collected. Miss Gross is somewhat recovered but is still a bit nervous. They are interviewed from 12:00 noon until about 3:30 p.m.

Miss Gross gives a statement saying that she met Fahey about three weeks earlier and had been on two dates with him. She met him through some mutual friends at the Meramec Canoe Club.

Peggy states that Fahey picked her up at her home around 6:30 p.m. on the 12th of August, taking her back to the house where he was staying. They had dinner with Mr. Chas. Peterson. They decided to attend the Outdoor Symphony Concert in Clayton. The concert got over around 11:00 p.m., and they went to a café called Alice & Hooky's on Olive Street Road. Miss Gross had three beers and Fahey had two.

They left the café about 12:15 a.m. on August 13th, and started back to Peggy's home. Fahey stopped the car on Warson Road in Clayton, about a block from Miss Gross' home, and they had been sitting there about ten minutes when two men walked up to their car.

Miss Gross continues to relate the story of their trip to Minnesota and being tied up near Champlin.

Peggy Gross is still quite nervous and very tired, so Agent Berens decides to continue the interview later.

It is decided that she should not return to the Nicollet Hotel, where the press may recognize her, so Agent Berens procures a room for her at the Curtis Hotel, 10th Street and 3rd Avenue South in Minneapolis.

Prior to proceeding to the hotel, Miss Gross requests that her brother John Gross in Chicago be called, and she is allowed to talk with him. She asks John to come to St. Paul to assist her. He says that he will start out right away.

Agent Berens accompanies Miss Gross to the Curtis Hotel. On the way, she requests to obtain the services of a physician to relieve her nerves. She is registered into room 420. The clerk is notified to not allow anyone to be admitted to her room and to prevent anyone other than those authorized to call her room.

Curtis Hotel

The hotel's house physician is sent to aid Miss Gross in her room. He gives her a sedative, and she sleeps from the late afternoon through the entire night.

The Curtis Hotel tabulated an invoice for $6.71 for services rendered.

•••

Daniel Cox Fahey, Jr. is interviewed by Special Agent Hardy, along with Minneapolis Police Detectives Arthur Dos Lauriers and Peter Uglem, and Deputy Sheriff Stanley Hurley, who supplies Hardy with a copy of the newspaper clipping shown to Miss Gross by the subjects during the trip to Minnesota.

Fahey states he was born November 5, 1906, at Washington, D.C., and is 31 years of age. He formerly lived at Hyattsville, Maryland. His mother, Catherine D. Fahey, lives at 4550 Connecticut Avenue in Washington, D.C. He is an only child. He graduated from Central School in Washington in 1924, and graduated from the University in Maryland in 1928, with a Bachelor of Science degree in landscape architecture. He got his Masters Degree in that subject in 1929. From 1929 to 1931 he practiced landscape architecture at 1435 K Street NW, in the Shannon and Luchs building in Washington, D.C. In 1931 he moved his business to 1701 Connecticut Avenue NW, where he maintained an office until 1936.

In 1933, he was employed by the National Parks Service at Washington as a landscape architect and Coordinator of Emergency Conservation work for the National Capital Parks and directed the activities of CCC Camps assigned to the Washington, D.C. area. He went to St. Louis on June 22, 1936, as Executive Officer for the Jefferson Expansion Memorial, which was a riverfront improvement project. He has a third floor office at 815 Olive Street in St. Louis, and his phone number is CENtral 8826. His salary is $3,800 yearly. He works under Supt. John L. Nagle of the Office of National Parks Service in St. Louis.

Fahey says that he has never been arrested, except for a speeding ticket in Washington. He is single, and resides at 19 Washington Terrace in St. Louis, which is the home of William C. Fordyce, Jr., a young lawyer in St. Louis. He has lived there since October 1937.

Fahey said, regarding Viola Cecelia "Peggy" Gross, that she is single and he had no knowledge that she was engaged to anyone. He met her within the past year at a party. On either Saturday July 23rd or 30th, he saw Miss Gross at The Canoe Club near Valley Park, Missouri. She was with Sewell Pangman. At that time Fahey was a guest of Mr. Babe O'Brien of St. Louis. He next saw her at a party on August 6th at Harry Langenberg, Jr.'s home at 49 Westmoreland Place, St. Louis. Peggy was with someone else at that time, and Fahey was by himself at this party. Langenberg was putting on a Midsummer Frolic, which was a Mexican themed party. Fahey talked with Miss Gross and others there. He phoned her the next day and made an engagement for Tuesday evening, August 9th.

On August 9th, at about 8 p.m., he met Miss Gross at her home at 10 Picardy Lane, which adjoins Warson Road in the subdivision of Clayton, Missouri. Fahey met her parents, and he and Peggy went to Alice & Hooky's Beer Garden on Olive Street Road in Fahey's car. There they spent the evening talking with two friends of Miss Gross'. Fahey took her back to her home at around 12:30 a.m.

Fahey describes his car as a Ford 1935 tan 4-door Deluxe Sedan with no trunk on the back, Motorola radio, 1938 Missouri plates 522-418, right rear light cracked, motor no. 18-82098, red wire wheels, green St. Louis city tax sticker on the lower right windshield under a AAA sticker.

1935 Ford Fordor Deluxe

He called Miss Gross on August 11th and made an engagement for them to have dinner the following evening.

He called on her at 6:30 p.m. on August 12th and they went to the Fordyce home for dinner. Charles Peterson, a friend of Fahey's, dined with them. Fahey and Miss Gross left the Fordyce home around 8:00 or 8:30 p.m. and went to a pop concert at Shaw Park in Clayton. They left the concert around 11:00 p.m. and went to Alice & Hooky's Beer Garden and stayed there until around midnight.

They then drove west on Olive Street Road to Warson Road and parked about a block from Miss Gross' house. They were parked there about ten minutes talking, with the lights on and the car facing south. Two men came up to the car and said, "This is a stickup." Fahey did not see any guns at first and stepped on the starter and started the car moving. One of the men hit him on the nose with the butt of a gun, and Fahey stopped the vehicle. Fahey's nose bled on and off until around 3:00 a.m.

Fahey goes on to tell his story of their abduction and transport to Minnesota with some detail, as he had been making mental notes all along the trip.

He mentions that he has only been in the Twin Cities once before, which was a three day period just a couple of months back in June, when he was sent by the National Park Service to attend a planning convention in Minneapolis. On that occasion, he traveled both ways by train, and stayed at the Nicollet Hotel.

Agent Hardy points out the similarities between the description Fahey gave of his captors to the description of Couch and Meredith supplied by the St. Louis Office. Fahey then recalls that John did say his name was John Couch.

Agents telephone the St. Louis office to have them airmail photos of Couch and Meredith to St. Paul.

They tell Fahey that he and Miss Gross will need to come in to look at the photos when they arrive the next day

Dan Fahey checks into a new room at the Ryan Hotel at 6th and Robert in St. Paul.

Ryan Hotel

•••

Special Agent E. N. Notesteen makes an inspection of the area where Fahey and Miss Gross were tied up off of Highway 169 near Champlin, Minnesota. His report includes:

Mr. Carl Gustafson, who was accompanied by Mr. R. C. Reilly, both of whom reside about two miles south of Champlin, were traveling near this area around 11:00 p.m. when they noticed a man standing in a wooded field crying for assistance. Fearing it might be a holdup, Gustafson informed Reilly to stay in the car, and if he did not return within ten minutes to come looking for him. Gustafson then proceeded toward the man who identified himself as Daniel Fahey of St. Louis, Missouri. Fahey's hands were tied behind his back, and his ankles were also bound. Gustafson loosened Fahey, who told him there was a young lady back further in the woods, who was also tied, and that he should go to her. Approximately fifteen minutes had passed, and Mr. Reilly appeared, and the three men go to release Miss Gross. Mr. Gustafson then took the victims to his home and he called the Sheriff's Office in Minneapolis.

•••

5:00 p.m.

Carl Fisher, a letter carrier from Sauk Center, Minnesota, calls the St. Paul FBI Office advising that he had seen a tan Ford Sedan with Missouri plates and red wire wheels parked in front of the Bar Harbor Night Club on the highway north of Brainerd.

About the same time, the St. Paul Police Department interviewed Frank McCauley, 347 Chestnut Street, St. Paul, who advised that he had seen a tan car with Missouri plates

Bar Harbor Night Club
Nisswa, Minnesota

522-418 parked in front of his home with two individuals who acted suspiciously. The police doubt parts of his story and note that the description of the car had been in the papers.

•••

St. Paul Agents notify FBI Director J. Edgar Hoover about the questioning of Fahey and Gross, and that they were initially trying to determine whether they had a legitimate complaint, or were making up the story for some reason.

The FBI was investigating the possibility that the kidnappers are Floyd Hamilton, the FBI's Public Enemy No. 1, and John Couch, sought by federal and state authorities. However, police broadcasts emanating from the Hennepin County Sheriff's office name Couch and his accomplice as a man identified as James Meredith.

Information obtained from James Clyde Reed, in jail at Kennett, Missouri, revealed that he always contacted Meredith by phone at FORest 8455, and that John Couch lived at 3742 Evans Street, in St. Louis. He added that both Couch and Meredith frequented Jim's Café.

Agents call Meredith's phone number and are able to determine that it was located at 5409 Maple Avenue in St. Louis, the home of Meredith's mother, Mrs. Grace O'Neal.

Agents start surveillance of Jim's Café and the vicinity of Taylor and Page Boulevard in St. Louis hoping to locate Couch and Meredith.

Agents proceed to 3742 Evans Avenue in St. Louis, and find Russell Couch, John's brother. Russell denies any knowledge of John's whereabouts or his activities. Russell is able to provide them with a list of relatives.

The agents proceed to the Missouri Baptist Hospital to interview John Couch's father, William Couch, at his work. He is also unable to provide any information on John's whereabouts, but is able to provide addresses for some of the relatives on the list provided by Russell.

•••

Newspaper reporters clamor to get what information they can on the abduction and release of Peggy Gross and Dan Fahey.

Questioned by reporters, Miss Gross answers questions with perfect poise. Her principal thought is for getting some clothes. Her dress was soiled when the kidnappers tied her in the woods south of Champlin, but she had it cleaned in Minneapolis this morning.

The gunmen took most of their money, except for $2, which they left in Fahey's wallet. Miss Gross managed to save Fahey's watch.

"I don't believe we were very frightened during the long ride to Minneapolis," Miss Gross says, "but now that it is all over, we've had time to think about the danger we were in, and to realize just what might have happened to us."

Carl Gustafson, in telling of finding Dan and Peggy said, "My automobile is noisy and I just managed to hear someone calling for help in the dark woods. I stopped the car and went over to where Fahey was standing on the other side of the fence. His hands were tied with wire behind his back and his feet were bound together."

"He yelled 'Please untie me,'" Gustafson said.

"I worked some time to release Fahey's hands, and then he asked me to go into the woods and look for Miss Gross."

"I found Miss Gross about 200 feet back into the woods. She was lying on the ground and had been bitten badly by mosquitoes. I got the wire off her and asked her how she felt."

"She told me, 'I have no feeling in my hands and arms, but outside of that I guess I'm all right.' She was shaky, but perked up quickly."

Harold Valley tells reporters that he also saw the car parked alongside the road. He said that he and his wife were driving from their home to Mississippi Beach, where they attended a neighborhood party.

The Valleys, who lives on the Brooklyn Center Road, about five miles from Champlin, turned off of Highway 169 and found a car nearly blocking the road. "There were four persons in the car," said Mrs. Valley. "Two in the front, and two in the back. The man in the front seat had a white shirt."

The Valleys didn't pay much attention, thinking that the people in the car were "spooners." One of the men had his back turned as if he were reaching into the back seat.

Fahey stated that he, "may not have acted very bravely about this, but when I think about what could have happened, it was perhaps better that we played ball."

"The only motive I can see for the kidnapping seems to be that the men wanted transportation to Minnesota. They treated us fairly well, but we only had a couple of hamburgers to eat on the way up here."

"Both seemed to have a great deal of money. When we stopped for gasoline, the men displayed a great amount of currency."

Miss Gross said that one of the men, who was called John, was surly, but that the one known as Jack was more pleasant.

S. J. Hardy, in control of the St. Paul office of the FBI during the absence of SAC Robert Hendon, is in charge of the investigation at present. Hendon is expected to return Monday. All federal agents in this district have been called in to aid with the investigation.

An automobile hubcap found by a St. Paul Dispatch reporter near the woods where the victims were discovered is turned over to the FBI for examination of fingerprints.

•••

Search continued today as a small army of peace officers from three states combed a 10 square mile area in the wilderness of extreme southwest Arkansas for Floyd Hamilton and a desperado companion believed to be Huron Ted Walters.

Hamilton and his companion fled to the thickly wooded section following a gun battle with Arkansas state police yesterday.

Texas, Oklahoma and Arkansas officers searched the area on foot and circled it in a revolving cordon of radio-equipped cars.

The area embraces the densely wooded mountain area along the Arkansas-Oklahoma border and the jungles of Cossatot River. The underbrush is so dense that visibility is limited to a few feet.

August 15, 1938

Monday

Weather: low of 67 at 5:00 a.m., high of 80 at 4:00 p.m.

Hennepin County authorities last night broadcast a warning to peace officers to watch for John Couch and James Meredith, Missouri ex-convicts. Their names were linked to the case when Miss Gross said one of her abductors had shown her a newspaper clipping about James Clyde Reed, now held on assault and robbery charges in Kennett, Missouri. Reed had told Kennett officers that he had been with Couch and Meredieth, but had parted from them not long before he was arrested in Blytheville, Arkansas.

•••

Peggy's brother John and their nephew John Murdock, arrive in the Twin Cities from Chicago, after driving all night.

The FBI decides to conclude the interviewing of Fahey and Miss Gross once they are able to review the photographs being sent from St. Louis.

Miss Gross, in the company of her brother John, goes to the St. Paul office for further questioning. It is noted that there are welts on her wrists from where they were tied with wire, and she says that her hands are numb and that she has no feeling in them. She also has many mosquito bites on her legs.

Miss Gross gives further statement, recalling a number of details since her previous interview on Sunday.

She gives detailed descriptions of her captors, which match the description given by Fahey, who is always interviewed separately.

When the photographs of Couch and Meredith arrive from St. Louis, they are placed with 36 other photos of people of similar size and nature.

Otis James Meredith   **John Couch**

The photos are first perused by Fahey, in the presence of SAC Hendon and Special Agent Hardy.

Fahey immediately and positively identifies the photo of Otis James Meredith as being "Jack." He partially and tentatively identifies the photo of John Couch as being "John."

The 38 photographs are then exhibited to Miss Gross, in the presence of SAC Hendon and Special Agents Hardy and Berens.

She likewise positively identifies Meredith, and partially identifies Couch.

Upon this determination, Miss Gross and Mr. Fahey prepare to depart for Chicago with John Gross around 2:00 p.m., but first they talk with reporters.

Spending Sunday and part of today with the FBI, they tell reporters they were unable to identify any pictures of known criminals as their abductors.

"Well it's certainly going to be something to talk about," said Miss Gross. "Was it a thrill? Well, now that it's over, I guess maybe it was."

Peggy Gross and Daniel Cox Fahey, Jr

She laughed when someone commented that she was a girl with a lot of nerve.

Fahey was not hesitant in adding, "She's a game girl."

Peggy told a reporter, "I wasn't really frightened until it was all over. While we were in the automobile we were so tense we did not realize how serious the situation was."

Miss Gross is wearing a new dress that she had bought earlier in the day. Fahey is wearing a shirt and trousers that he has borrowed from an FBI agent.

Peggy and Dan leave for Chicago by automobile with Peggy's brother John and nephew John Murdock, where they will catch a plane back to St. Louis.

Meanwhile, small town bankers throughout the area are taking extra precautions against bandits, fearing the kidnappers may be short of money, and may attempt a bank robbery.

•••

Earlier today, St. Louis Police were called to a restaurant at 4044 North Grand Boulevard. There, the attendant and two customers told of a hurried departure a short time before of two men who they thought to be Couch and Meredith. The two had ordered coffee and a soft drink but left without finishing them. The restaurant attendant and the two customers said the men resembled newspaper pictures of Couch and Meredith.

•••

11:29 a.m.

Mr. Rose, assistant to the Assistant Secretary of the Treasury, telephones the FBI Headquarters in Washington, D.C., advising that he has just received a telephone call from his wife to the effect that her cousin, who has been employed on the Jefferson Memorial in St. Louis, was abducted along with his date, and driven to Minnesota. The boy's mother is very anxious to know what has happened to her son and inquired as to whether the Bureau has any knowledge of this matter.

Mr. Rose was advised that Fahey is safe and should be returning to St. Louis soon. At this point, the kidnappers have not been caught nor has Fahey's car been recovered.

•••

St. Louis Special Agents go to the home of Meredith's mother, Grace O'Neal, at 5409 Maple Avenue in St. Louis. Mrs. O'Neal is in physical distress, has gone without sleep and is extremely nervous. They explain the reason for their visit and ask for her cooperation, whichshe obliges, saying it would be best for everyone if Otis were captured soon.

She says that Otis has a wife named Vera, who is working in a tavern in Effie, Minnesota. She does not remember Vera's maiden name, but that they got married several years earlier when Otis was working for the CCC Camp near Effie. She added that they have a daughter who was three years old last January.

Grace remembered that Otis and Vera lived in Minneapolis for a while at 2801 Portland Avenue. Later, they both came and stayed at her house for several weeks, but Vera did not like St. Louis and returned to her father's home in Effie. She has not heard from Vera since.

Grace provides the agents with names and addresses of Otis' relatives and promises that she will try to ascertain his whereabouts. She says that she will call the St. Louis FBI office if she hears any information about her son.

•••

FBI surveillance of Jim's Café in St. Louis continues today in hopes of sighting Couch and Meredith. Waitress Florence Scott tells agents that she is well acquainted with Couch and Meredith, and that they had frequented the establishment quite often this summer, but that she had not seen them for the past couple of weeks.

Grace O'Neal

•••

Russell Couch is interviewed again by the FBI at his home, but he is intoxicated and unable to furnish any information of value.

•••

Midafternoon, the St. Paul FBI Office receives a telegram from the St. Louis Office advising that Meredith had at one time lived in Minneapolis at 2801 Portland Avenue and that his wife Vera works as a waitress in a tavern in Effie, Minnesota. It is deemed advisable to send Agents S. W. Hardy and R. T. Noonan immediately to Effie and also to check on the address on Portland Avenue.

Agent Berens goes to 2801 Portland Avenue in Minneapolis and there interviews Mrs. Robertson. She operates a rooming house at this location. She said that Meredith had lived there about one year, and that he was employed at William Bros Boiler in Minneapolis. Mrs. Robertson says that Meredith left a year ago last spring and went to St. Louis with his wife Vera. She states that Vera returned to her family's home back in Effie shortly after going to St. Louis.

She goes on to tell how Meredith met Vera while working at a CCC Camp near her home. She also recalls that Vera had a very good friend in Minneapolis in Mrs. Bieker, who operates a rest home some place on Portland Avenue and that Vera had visited her recently.

SA Berens calls the Hennepin County Medical Association and the City License Bureau, but fails to find any reference to a Mrs. Bieker.

Inquiry at a rest home on Portland Avenue discloses that Mrs. Bieker now operates the Third Avenue Rest Home at 1807 Third Avenue South, in Minneapolis.

Berens checks at this address but does not find Mrs. Bieker. He does get her telephone number, however, ATLantic 0038.

Mrs. Bieker is telephoned, but the nature of the visit is not discussed with her or her husband. Special Agent Berens visits both of them at their apartment at 2301 10th Avenue South in Minneapolis. Mrs. Bieker says that she is a very close friend to Vera, but that she will cooperate fully in the apprehension of Meredith.

Mrs. Bieker states that at one time Meredith worked in St. Louis in a bakery and also thought he may have worked in a hospital as an orderly. She said that Vera had gone to St. Louis with Meredith, but returned to Minneapolis after a short there and worked for her for a period before returning to her family in Effie. She adds that she knew that Vera had received a letter from her husband about April or May of this year. She says that Meredith thought quite a lot of his daughter, Deloris. Mrs. Bieker states that though they are separated, Vera and Meredith are not divorced. She says that Vera now lives with her father, Charles Rootes, on a farm nine miles east of Effie, Minnesota, on Highway One. She says that Mr. Rootes works at the CCC Camp a short distance from his home, where Meredith had been enrolled.

Mrs. Bieker knows little of Meredith's family, other than that he has a brother, Leon, who lives in St. Louis, and that his mother had visited the Rootes' at Effie, Minnesota. Meredith's mother is known to the Biekers as Grace Sellers.

Mrs. Bieker adds that while Meredith worked at the CCC Camp, he always sent money to his mother, and that he seemed to be quite a decent lad.

While living in Minneapolis, Jack had purchased a 1929 Model A Ford from the River Lake Motors Company. He later sold the car to get money to live on while they moved back to St. Louis.

Mrs. Bieker is of the opinion that some of the difficulties experienced by Meredith was occasioned in part by Vera, as she often persuaded him to do things that he did not want to do, or prevented him from doing things that he wanted to do. At one time, Meredith wanted to take up diesel engineering work, but Vera dissuaded him, claiming it was too great an expense.

SA Berens also interviews Vincent Eychaner, Mrs. Bieker's brother-in-law, who had served in the CCC Camp with Meredith. He states that Meredith was a fairly decent chap, and that he knew nothing wrong with him or against him. He said that Meredith was fond of fishing and knew the country around Effie quite well, having fished in a number of lakes in that vicinity. Meredith had gone to Big Falls, Minnesota, fishing on the Big Fork River, and also fished at Deer Lake and Long Lake.

Berens asks Eychaner about Charles Rootes, to which Vincent replies that Charles was working at the CCC Camp at the time he was there and was a reputable individual.

Two snapshots of Meredith are obtained from Mrs. Bieker. Since these are more recent photographs of Meredith than the St. Louis Police Department photos, they are retained in the files of the St. Paul Office.

•••

Agents check on Meredith's employment history at the William Bros Boiler Company. Meredith had been employed as a press punch operator for about one year, and he left this employment about May 1936, having received an injury for which he was treated at St. Mary's Hospital. They believe it was a hernia. The company had very little additional information on Meredith, other than he formerly worked for the Washburn Crosby Company flourmill in Minneapolis.

•••

Floyd Hamilton and Huron Ted Walters have eluded another police trap today.

Officers from Oklahoma, Louisiana, Texas, and Arkansas believed they had Hamilton and Walters surrounded in the area near DeQueen Arkansas yesterday, but a 24 hour search failed to disclose their hiding place. Rain hampered the work of bloodhounds brought here from the Oklahoma Penitentiary at McAlester.

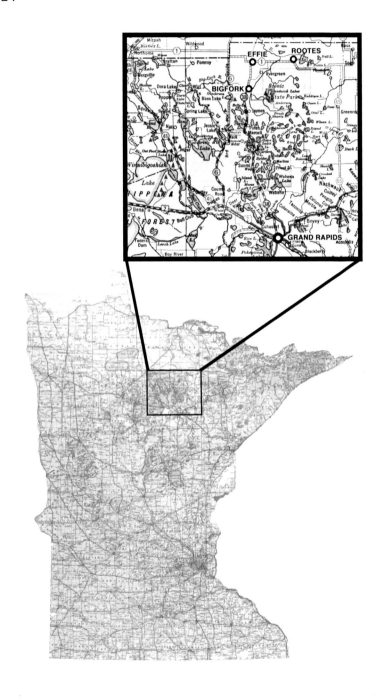

•••

2:00 p.m.

    Special Agents S. W. "Sam" Hardy and R. T. Noonan depart for Effie, Minnesota, with appropriate equipment.

6:00 p.m.

    The agents arrive in Grand Rapids, Minnesota, the seat for Itasca County in which Effie is located. They discover that Sheriff Elmer Madson and Chief Deputy Litchke are not in town at this time.
    The agents call SAC Hendon in St. Paul, who gives them further background on Meredith. His wife lives with her family on the Charles Rootes farm nine miles east of Effie, that the Charles Rootes family is reputable, and Meredith was friendly with a neighbor named Frank Bieker, with whom Meredith worked at the CCC Camp at Deer Lake. Meredith met Vera while working in this camp. Charles Rootes is employed at this CCC Camp. This information came from an informant that thought that Meredith would not contact his wife, but would fish and hide out around Long Lake or Deer Lake north of Grand Rapids.
    On receiving this information, Agents Hardy and Noonan proceed north to Bigfork, Minnesota, which is about 15 miles from the Rootes Farm. There they locate Chief of Police Glen Miller. The Agents instruct Miller to contact Itasca County Deputy Sheriff Harry Lamson of Effie. The four officers meet at the town hall in Bigfork around 8:30 p.m. The agents exhibit photographs of Couch and Meredith to Lamson and Miller, both of whom knew Charles Rootes and Jack Meredith.

Police Chief Glen Miller   **Deputy Harry Lamson**

Miller and Lamson notify their families that they are going on an investigation.

Agent Noonan drives the officers to the Charles Rootes Farm. En route, Agent Hardy puts together a pump shotgun and a .351 rifle. He loads the shotgun and clips for the rifle.

As they approach the Rootes home, the plan is for Noonan to drive past the farm so that the officers can see the location of the house in relation to other buildings. About 9:20 p.m., Noonan drives past the Rootes home. Although the sun has set, the officers are able to make an observation because there are two cars in the yard near the house, and one of them has its headlights on. There are several people in the yard around the cars.

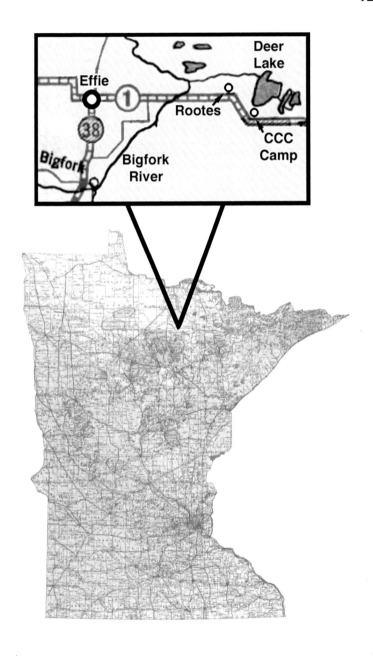

They continue to drive about a quarter of a mile to a point where the car can be turned around without anyone observing the turn. On the way back to the Rootes' driveway, it is decided that Noonan will drive immediately behind the car with its headlights on. Agent Noonan and Chief Miller are to get out of the Bureau car on the left side, and cover everybody on the left side of that vehicle. Agent Hardy and Deputy Lamson are to get out on the right, and cover everyone on the right and in front of the car.

Noonan and Lamson carry .38 revolvers. Miller has his .32 revolver, and Agent Hardy has a .38 service revolver and the shotgun. The .351 rifle lay on the seat of the Bureau car, and Hardy has the clips for it, in case Couch and Meredith get out of the range of the shotgun.

Rootes House

As they pull into the driveway, the officers note the Missouri license plates on a tan Ford. Agent Hardy yells out, "There's the Missouri car now, 522-418." Noonan skids to a stop directly behind Fahey's car. The officers exit the car quickly and recognize Couch and Meredith standing in front of the car, cleaning fish by the headlights with one of the Rootes boys.

Meredith's wife is nearby next to the farmhouse.

Agent Hardy calls out, "We're Federal Officers. You are under arrest. Put up your hands."

Couch runs from in front of the Fahey car to the right front door where Deputy Lamson and Agent Noonan meet him with their guns drawn. Lamson and Noonan shout for him to put his hands up. Couch put his hands in the air, in obvious fear. Couch was trying to make a grab for the two loaded pistols in the glove box of the car, which had its windows rolled down.

At the same time that Couch lunged toward the car, Meredith started running out into the darkness towards the underbrush, and the officers yell at him to stop. He keeps running and Agent Hardy fires one shot at him with his shotgun. The buckshot hits him in the back. He has run approximately 20 yards from where he stood cleaning fish, and officer Hardy shot from a point about ten yards further away, making the distance of the shot about 30 yards. As Meredith starts to fall, Chief Miller shoots at him once with the .32 revolver, and hits him in the left thigh.

"Meredith glanced at the officers approaching with drawn guns, and ran towards the woods," said Deputy Lamson. "Several shots were fired and Meredith fell to the ground."

"Meredith was just getting out of Fahey's car when we arrived," Bigfork Police Chief Glen Miller stated. "He started to run towards a chicken coop about 60 feet away. I shot him by the rays of my flashlight. Apparently one of the federal men fired at him also with a shotgun."

Noonan and Miller run over to where Meredith is lying with his hands up, and he yells, "Don't shoot. You've got me. I give up."

Meredith's wife Vera comes running toward him. Meredith tries to rise and falls back to the ground. "Why did you kill the father of my baby?" Vera cries as she bends over Jack's body. The officers inform her that he is not dead.

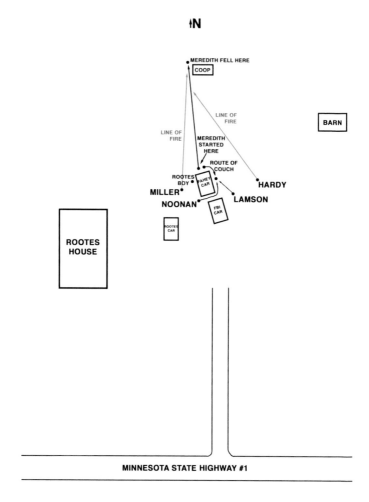

Meredith is led back to the Fahey car with the assistance of the officers, and Noonan and Miller search him for weapons, finding none. He is then handcuffed.

Couch is also searched, finding no weapons. Miller finds the key to the Fahey car in his left pants pocket. Hardy asks Couch, "Where are your guns?" Couch replies, "In the car." Hardy holds his gun on Couch, and asks Miller to search the car. Miller finds two loaded nickel-plated revolvers in the glove compartment. One is a Harrington and Richardson .32 caliber with black rubber grips, which contained six bullets. The other a Smith and Wesson .32 Caliber revolver with black rubber grips. This gun has one cartridge in it, which is in the chamber, ready to be fired.

Couch is asked by the officers, "are these your guns?" Couch replies, "Yes."

Roy Rootes and Glen Miller next to the chicken coop in the area where Meredith was shot

132

"Are there any more guns that you have at this place?"

"No," Couch replies.

Agent Hardy, in the presence of Meredith and members of the Rootes family, asks Couch, "Were you the men who kidnapped Fahey and Gross in Clayton, Missouri, and forced them to come in this car to Minnesota?"

Couch replies, "Yes."

Hardy asks, "Did you leave them tied up with wire down near Minneapolis?"

Couch says, "Yes we did. We can't deny it because you've caught us with their car in our possession for proof."

Hardy then asks, "Was this Meredith with you when you kidnapped Fahey and Miss Gross?"

Couch says, "Yes, he was. We did it."

Hardy then asks Couch, "You two were shooting at officers in a gun battle down in Texas near Fort Worth about ten day ago, too, weren't you?"

Couch replies, "Yes, we were."

Couch is then handcuffed and chained.

Meredith is searched further, and on him are found a black leather pocketbook containing $5.84, a roll of black wire, a penknife, an Independent Lock Co. key #77879, a .32 caliber cartridge, and a "Good Luck" medal.

•••

Virginia Lund, who was 8 year-old "Budge" Walls in 1938, recalls the incident, which took place directly across the road from the Walls' farm.

I can remember that like it was yesterday.

My sister and I played with Jack Meredith's daughter when we were little. She had the nickname, "Smoky," because she would sneak cigarette butts and smoke them.

The Rootes boys would come over often and sleep in the haymow of our barn with my brothers. They were there the night of the shooting. We all heard the shots. The Rootes boys got up and ran home. We all ran out into our pasture, and I was watching. The cops were there and they had their lights on them. They had shot Jack Meredith and captured Johnny Couch. That was a lot of excitement back then.

•••

Meredith is put in Fahey's car by Agent Noonan and Chief Miller so that they can take him to the nearest doctor, which is Dr. James H. Bender in Bigfork. On the way to Bigfork, the officers asks him why he ran when he was ordered to put up his hands. Meredith replies, "It was an impulse to make a break to get away."

Agent Hardy and Deputy Lamson take Couch to Bigfork in the Bureau car, where the St. Paul office is notified by phone at 10:03 p.m.

Couch is then taken by Hardy and Lamson to the Itasca County Jail in Grand Rapids, Minnesota. En route, Couch tells Deputy Lamson that after he and Meredith tied up Gross and Fahey in the woods near Champlin, they, "went back to Minneapolis to meet a friend, but things looked too hot for us there, so we had to head for the north woods."

They arrive at the jail at about 11:30 p.m. Couch is searched again, and incarcerated therein. They find on him a piece of paper on which was written "752 Bayard" and "Mulcahy." Couch states that this was an acquaintance of his from the Missouri Penitentiary, from whom he had intended to borrow money. They also find two pages of a song that Couch had written in pencil.

After being brought into Dr. Bender's office in Bigfork, Meredith asks, "How long were they tied up before they were found?" referring to Peggy and Dan.

Agent Noonan tells him that Fahey had attracted a farmer's attention late that night.

"Good," Meredith replied.

Meredith then states, "It's a losing game, you can't win."

Noonan inquires as to why they took Fahey and Miss Gross with them when they stole their car. Meredith replies, "That was one way to make a getaway, and we figured it was best." He adds that, "Fahey was sure tough, and tried to protect the girl."

Meredith asks the officer where they got the tip that he and Couch were in Effie.

Noonan replies that it was because of his past connections there.

Meredith says that the government knows all about both he and Couch, and that they were being sought on a similar offense in St. Louis.

Agent Noonan asks Meredith if he and Couch had robbed any banks, to which he replies, "No."

Meredith tells Agent Noonan, " I'm done for," to which Dr. Bender replies that he might not be hurt so seriously. Meredith states that he wishes that the shot had hit him higher in the back, "so it would be all over now."

Dr. Bender tries to reassure him again, but Meredith says, "I can can feel the injury moving toward my heart."

Meredith is able to point out where the bullet from Chief Miller's pistol hit him. Portions of the copper casing from the bullet are removed from the edge of the wound.

Meredith tells the officers that his wife and three year old daughter live at the Rootes farm, and that he had just come back for a visit with them. He also tells them he worked at the CCC Camp near there about three years ago.

Dr. Bender feels that Meredith should be placed in a hospital right away and that an emergency operation should be performed.

Around 10:30 p.m., a bed is made out of pillows and blankets in the back of the Fahey car and Noonan and Miller take Meredith to the Itasca County Hospital in Grand Rapids, Minnesota, about 40 miles from Bigfork.

Itasca Hospital

They arrive in Grand Rapids around 11:30 p.m. Dr. Bender arrives at the hospital separately with Dr. J. L. McLeod of the Itasca Clinic in Grand Rapids. Dr. McLeod is also a sitting State Senator.

X-rays are taken in an attempt to locate the cause of Meredith's rapid decline.

•••

Late in the night of August 15th, Lieut. T. P. Winborne of the Effie CCC Camp telephones the St. Paul FBI Office that he has confidential information that Couch and Meredith are located on a farm near the camp. The two had already been apprehended by this time, but Winborne is not informed of this.

•••

11:10 p.m.

SAC Robert Hendon in St. Paul contacts the FBI Headquarters in Washington, D.C., and reports to Assistant FBI Director P. E. Foxworth, as Director J. Edgar Hoover is in New York. He states that he has just received a call from Special Agent Hardy in Bigfork:

SA Hardy, in company with SA Noonan, Glen Miller, Chief of Police in Bigfork, and Harry Lamson, a Deputy Sheriff from Effie, Minn., went to Charley Roote's farm home near Effie. As they approached this place they saw two cars, and recognized one of them as the victim's car in this case. SA Hardy immediately jumped out and called upon Couch and Meredith to submit to arrest, announcing himself as a Federal officer. Couch submitted to arrest, but Meredith ran across a field and it was necessary for SA Hardy to shoot him with buckshot to stop him.

Assistant Director Foxworth makes a report to Hoover in New York:

Couch has admitted the kidnaping, the theft of the car, and the gun battle in Texas. Their loaded pistols were found in the car. Meredith was at once taken to Dr. James Bender in Bigfork, and will be taken to a hospital in Grand Rapids. It is not known how seriously he is hurt as yet, but Agent Hardy when talking to Mr. Hendon seemed to think he would live. The US Attorney has authorized a complaint. Mr. Hendon stated that no one but those participating and the doctor knows of this happening yet. I advised Mr. Hendon that I would call him back in a short time.

P.E. Foxworth
Assistant Director of the FBI.

August 16, 1938

Tuesday

12:05 a.m.

FBI Headquarters in Washington calls Special Agent in Charge Hendon in St. Paul and asks him if there is any danger of this matter leaking out. Hendon states that since Agent Hardy's phone calls to him had to pass through three small town switchboards, and because the people of the farm knew about it, and because some in town saw them come in, he doubted the news could be kept quiet.

Washington starts to prepare a press release.

•••

12:30 a.m.

Dr. Bender and Dr. McLeod finish up X-raying Meredith. Around 1:30 a.m., they make the decision to operate, as they presume that he will probably be dead by morning if an operation is not performed due to internal bleeding. They also feel that the chances are about 95% to 5% that he may die anyway even if the operation is performed.

2:30 a.m.

Meredith is placed on the operating table and ether is administered by Dr. Meyer at 2:47 a.m. The incision and actual operation begin shortly thereafter.

Around 3:30 a.m. a bullet is removed from the back of Meredith, just under the skin. This bullet is given to Agent Noonan. Three buckshot wounds are also treated, and the mesentery is sutured.

The surgery concludes around 3:45 a.m.

Meredith is removed from the operating room around 4:15 a.m., and he starts coming out of the ether at 5:45 a.m.

Shortly after coming around, Meredith gives his age as 26; date of birth, June 30, 1912, at Glenwood, Arkansas; and the name of his mother, Mrs. Grace O'Neal, 5409 Maple Avenue, St. Louis, Missouri; her phone number being FORest 8455.

•••

John Murdock•John Gross•Peggy Gross• Daniel Fahey

Miss Gross and Mr. Fahey arrive in Chicago early in the morning, driven there by her brother John and his nephew. Peggy sleeps for a couple of hours in the apartment of Mrs. Rene G. Le Brosi in the Parkway Hotel, then departs with Fahey on an American Airlines plane for St. Louis at about 8:40 a.m.

"About an hour after she left, we were notified that two men had been arrested as the kidnappers," said Mrs. Le Brosi.

•••

It appears that Meredith may not pull through, so SA Hardy telephones Deputy Lamson in Effie, so that he can get Meredith's wife to the hospital to see him before he dies.

J. Edgar Hoover issues telegrams of appreciation to
Chief Miller and Deputy Lamson:

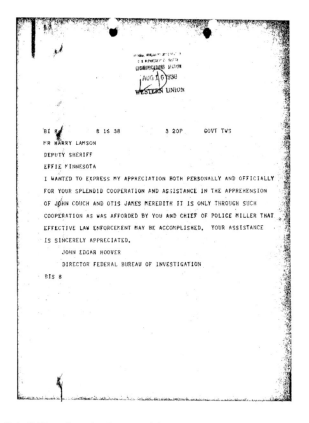

SAC Hendon in St. Paul instructs Agent Hardy to give
Officers Lamson and Miller $10 each for their aid and
assistance.

Hendon informs Washington that newspaper reporters
and photographers will probably storm the hospital where
Meredith is being treated, and he has instructed his agents to
hold him incommunicado.

•••

8:15 a.m.

SAC Hendon in St. Paul telephones SAC Norris in St. Louis to inform him of the capture of Couch and Meredith the evening before.

•••

US District Attorney Victor Anderson files kidnapping complaints against Couch and Meredith, charging them with kidnapping under the "Lindbergh Law," which provides for the death penalty in cases where kidnap victims are injured in the commission of the crime. Daniel Cox Fahey, Jr. was hit on the nose with the butt of a gun when he was first abducted.

Anderson says that he will demand $100,000 bail for each prisoner when they are brought to St. Paul for arraignment, but the time for arraignment has not been set because of Meredith's condition.

•••.

Cameramen and reporters from the daily papers in the Twin Cities and Duluth swarm to Effie, Minnesota, to interview the Rootes family, as well as Deputy Lamson and Chief Glen Miller.

Doris, Roy, Luther and Carl
Charles, Vera, Deloris and Gladys Rootes

Charles Rootes relates the story of Couch and Meredith coming to his farm. "Meredith drove into the farm yard Sunday morning with Couch. It was the first time Vera had seen Meredith since separating from him in St. Louis two years ago."

"I wondered where they got the good looking car because they only had $5 in cash and very few belongings. But I didn't realize they had stolen the car."

"They fished Sunday and puttered around. The officers suddenly appeared Monday, as Couch was cleaning fish by the headlights of the automobile. There was a lot of noise and it was all over. We found out that Meredith was wanted."

Dr. James H. Bender   **Dr. J. Lawrence McLeod**

10:30 a.m.

Drs. J. H. Bender and J. L. McLeod file a report as to Meredith's condition:

Jack Meredith was brought to the Itasca Hospital, Grand Rapids, Minnesota, around 11:30 p.m., August 15th. He had wounds from one .32 caliber bullet, which was imbedded in the gluteal muscles, and from three large buckshot, one of which had passed under the skin of the left side and escaped. The second traveled up under the skin and was removed from the side of the chest. The third had penetrated the abdomen rupturing the kidney and tearing the mesentery, causing extensive hemorrhage.
The man was in surgical shock. He was given intravenal fluids, and after X-ray was operated upon by the undersigned. The kidney and mesenteric wounds were sutured and bleeding stopped.
Meredith's condition remains critical at this time.

J. L. McLeod, M.D.
J. H. Bender, M.D.

•••

Special Agent J. S. Bush of the St. Louis Office tries to locate the "Mulcahy" whose name and address were found on Couch at the time of his arrest. Mulcahy served time in the Missouri State Penitentiary with Couch.

SA Bush goes to 752 Bayard Avenue and interviews W. F. Commerford. Commerford states that Del Mulcahy, approximately 28 years of age, rents a room at this address and has lived here for about four months with his wife Louise. Mulcahy drives a truck for a living and is not present at this time. SA Bush will return at a later date to attempt to question Mulcahy.

•••

Couch is questioned as to where they got the pistols, and he replies that they were Meredith's, and that Meredith has had these weapons since early in July, and that both of them had used each gun.

When Meredith is questioned about the pistols, he says that he and Couch stole them on jobs that they had pulled.

•••

10:55 a.m.

     FBI Director Hoover sends a copy of a press memo his office has prepared to Gordon Dean, an Executive Assistant in the Attorney General's Office, who also handles their media relations.

J. Edgar Hoover

146

*Memorandum to Mr. Gordon Dean, Special Executive
Assistant to the Attorney General
From: J. Edgar Hoover, Director of the FBI*

*I am transmitting herewith a memorandum to the apprehension
of Otis James Meredith and John Couch by Special Agents of
the Federal Bureau of Investigation, which I thought you might
like to relay to the press.*

*Very truly yours,
John Edgar Hoover
Director*

For   **UNITED STATES DEPARTMENT**
Immediate   **OF JUSTICE**
Release   **August 16, 1938**

**It is announced today by the Department of Justice that
Special Agents of the Federal Bureau of Investigation,
assisted by local officers, last night apprehended Otis
James Meredith and John Couch near Effie, Minnesota, on
the farm of Charlie Rootes, the father-in-law of Meredith.
At the time the subjects were placed under arrest by
Special Agents of the FBI, Meredith resisted and
endeavored to escape, he was shot and wounded and is now
receiving medical attention at Grand Rapids, Minnesota.**

**John Couch is presently being held at the jail in Grand
Rapids, Michigan** (sic). **Couch and Meredith were
identified from photographs yesterday by Daniel Cox
Fahey, Jr., and Viola Gross as being the two individuals
who had kidnapped them at Clayton, Missouri, on the night
of August 12, 1938, thereafter commandeered Fahey's car
and transported the victims to Minneapolis,**

Minnesota, where they were bound and left along a roadside. The automobile of Fahey was found in the possession of Couch and Meredith at the time of their arrest.

When questioned by Special Agents of the FBI, John Couch admitted his participation in the kidnapping and also implicated Meredith. Couch further admitted the theft of a 1934 Buick Sedan in Greenwood, Missouri, on July 29, 1938.

This sedan was abandoned in Fort Worth, Texas, on the night of August 6 after Couch and Meredith had a running gun fight with local officers on the highway between Dallas and Fort Worth, which is admitted by Couch. A federal complaint was filed at Fort Worth, Texas, on August 11, 1938, by Special Agents of the FBI charging Couch and Meredith with violation of the Federal Kidnapping Act.

John Couch was received at the Missouri State Penitentiary, Jefferson, Missouri, on June 8, 1933, from Cooper County, Missouri to serve a sentence of nine years for the crime of auto theft. He was conditionally released on June 9, 1938.

James Otis Meredith, according to the criminal record on file in the Federal Bureau of Investigation, was received at the Missouri State Penitentiary, Jefferson City, Missouri, July 10, 1929, From Pulaski County, Missouri, to serve five years on a charge of burglary and larceny. He was paroled on September 20, 1930, the parole being revoked on March 30, 1931. Meredith was arrested by the St. Louis Police Department on October 27, 1930, upon a charge of attempted robbery. He was thereafter sentenced to serve five years in the Missouri State Reformatory, Boonville, Missouri.

Gordon Dean

Around noon, Gordon Dean replies to Hoover's memo:

Memorandum for Mr. J. Edgar Hoover, Director,
Federal Bureau of Investigation
From: Gordon Dean, Special Executive Assistant to the
Attorney General

Attached are five copies of the release, which was issued at
11:45 this morning to the press.

Very truly yours,
Gordon Dean
Special Executive Assistant to the Attorney General

(The copies of the press release are identical to the release sent to Mr. Dean by Hoover.)

•••

Shortly after replying to Hoover's memo regarding the press release, Gordon Dean fires off another memo to the FBI Director:

Memorandum for Mr. J. Edgar Hoover, Director, Federal Bureau of Investigation

From Gordon Dean, Special Executive Assistant to the Attorney General

This morning at approximately 11 o'clock I received from you the proposed press release dealing with the capture of Otis James Meredith and John Couch who were wanted on charges of kidnapping. The proposed release, unchanged, was immediately sent to the Mimeograph Room and at 11:45 a.m. it was distributed to the press. Several times during the morning I had received inquiries in which newspapermen inquired whether there was any break in the case and whether any captures had been made. I informed them that we had nothing as of yet to report.

Just a few minutes after one of these conversations, and before the press release had been returned from the Mimeograph Room, the Washington Daily News was on the street carrying the story in headlines with a St. Paul dateline. At the time that I called the Washington Times they had the story in full from St. Paul, Minnesota. In other words, the story was not in any real sense released from Washington, nor was it by any stretch of the imagination released simultaneously at St. Paul and Washington. The story broke from St. Paul. The story was, of course, one of national interest, as is every kidnaping case. If there are any questions on this point the answer is found in the streamers with which the Washington News, at a distance of some 1,500 miles, featured the story. Of course, if releases are issued in this manner it is quite obvious that if the Attorney General wished to make any change in them it would be impossible for him to do so. Furthermore such procedures would seem contrary to the clear understanding which we reached with the Attorney General on this subject some months ago.

Very truly yours,

Gordon Dean
Special Executive Assistant to the Attorney General

•••

11:50 a.m.

Meredith gives his statement to the FBI from his hospital bed:

<u>UNSIGNED STATEMENT OF MEREDITH</u>

Grand Rapids, Minn.
August 16, 1938
11:50 A.M.

I, James Otis Meredieth, realize that I am about to die, give this statement willingly to S. W. Hardy, Special Agent, Federal Bureau of Investigation, and Dr. J. L. McLeod and Miss Mabel Korsell, Supt. Of Itasca Hospital at Grand Rapids, Minn., of my own free will.
About 2:00 A.M., Saturday morning, John Couch and I kidnaped Daniel C. Fahey and Miss Gross on Warson Road in Clayton, Mo. They were parked in the front seat of this same tan Ford V8 car with Missouri license that I had at my

father-in-law's house last night, Aug. 15, 1938, when I was arrested. My father-in-law is Charles Rootes, and he lives 9 miles east of Effie, Minnesota. Couch and I each had revolvers. Couch hit Fahey with his pistol and cut his nose. It bled.

Couch and I told Miss Gross and Fahey that it was a stickup, and that they would have to go along with us. Then Couch and I made Miss Gross and Fahey ride in the back seat and we drove them from Clayton, Mo., to a point north of Minneapolis a few miles. We made them go with us. There, Couch and I tied them up with wire and left them in a field. We stole Fahey's car. They did not go with us voluntarily. We made them go with us. We did not release them until we got to Minneapolis because we wanted a car to come up to Minnesota and if we had let them go they would have contacted the police right away. We stole money out of Fahey's pocketbook. Fahey tried to protect Miss Gross. He said if I would put my gun away he would whip me. I think he would have done so, too.

I served a prison sentence at Jefferson City, Mo., Penitentiary for attempted robbery.

Couch and I stole a car in Missouri, in some little town, a Buick car, last month, July 1938, and then we picked up two girl hitchhikers. The officers chased us between Fort Worth and Dallas, Texas, and Couch and I were shooting at the officers with .38 pistols. In Texas we escaped from the officers, but they captured the girls and got the car Couch and I had stolen.

After leaving Fahey and Miss Gross in the field near Minneapolis tied up with wire about quarter of ten, Saturday night, Aug. 13. We bought the wire we used to tie them with in a hardware store in southern Minnesota. Couch made the loops in the wire in the car while we were going along so the wire was all ready to use when we got to the place where we tied and left Miss Gross and Fahey.

After tying up Fahey and Miss Gross, Couch and I drove to Effie, Minnesota. We still had our revolvers with us. At Chas. Rootes' home 9 miles east of Effie, we visited with my wife. My wife has been separated from me for two years. We took Fahey's car to the Rootes home and had our pistols. When the officers came to the Rootes' home last night they told us they were Federal officers, that we were under arrest and for us to put up our hands. I knew there was a federal warrant out for me so I resisted arrest and tried to get away.

(Unsigned)

Witnesses:
S.W. Hardy, Sp. Agt.
F.B.I. St. Paul, Minn
J. Lawrence McLeod
Mabel Korsell

Peggy Gross and Daniel C. Fahey, Jr. arrive at Lambert-St. Louis Field by airplane from Chicago. They are met by Peggy's fiancé Sewell Pangman, her father Robert H. Gross, and her sister Adelaide.

Before they leave the airport, they answer questions for reporters.

"The man who was called Jack in our hearing, made himself very agreeable," Miss Gross told reporters.

"He asked me my address, saying he was going to send me a postcard from every town he stopped. Then he said, 'We're coming back to St. Louis and take the police by storm. We don't like those St. Louis police.'"

"Jack seemed to have a lot of money. He would take bills from a roll of fives, with some twenties, to pay for the things we bought." Miss Gross said.

"He apologized repeatedly for having to tie me up, saying I was a 'swell kid' and he let me put a handkerchief over my ankles before he bound the wire around. I had on Dan's coat, and I pulled the sleeves down over my wrists before he wired them. He shook hands with Dan saying to him, 'you're not a bad guy.' The latter part of the ride they were calling us Dan and Peggy."

"I asked him if he ever went to college, and he said 'No, only the sixth grade in school.'"

"I was frightened as to what might happen, rather than afraid of the two men."

Fahey said, "We did not know where they were taking us until, after riding for some time, we saw we were northbound on Highway 61. We made only a few stops, for gasoline and food. Couch would step out and brings us food, as good as could be had along the road."

Fahey added, "When Peggy and I had a chance to talk quietly, I advised her to start crying and see what effect that would have. She had some difficulty getting the tears started, but when she started, she was soon really weeping and couldn't stop. There was no effect on the men, as all they said to her was, 'Shut up!'"

"They grew more friendly as the trip progressed, and by the time we came near Minneapolis, it was almost like a picnic. As we drove through the outskirts of the city after dark, they said they had a job to pull at 11:00 p.m., and asked us, apparently meaning it, if we would like to go along. If we didn't, we would have to be tied up and left somewhere. The latter was what we chose."

"When they stopped the car and let us out, I went around and got the pliers out of the toolkit in the car for them to use on the wire. I had no wire in the car, but they had some, which looked like picture wire."

"We climbed a fence and went into the woods, and they talked to us in a friendly way as they bound us. I put my feet together and held my knees apart so I would have a little play in moving my legs, which I found useful after they left us. They tied a handkerchief over my mouth. They didn't gag Peggy, but warned her not to cry out for an hour."

•••

Special Agent A. G. Berens files an official FBI Complaint:

On 08-13-38 in Clayton, St. Louis, Missouri, Otis James Meredith and John Couch unlawfully did seize, kidnap and hold...Daniel Cox Fahey, Jr., a resident of St. Louis, Missouri...in possession of...1935 Ford V-8 Deluxe Sedan, Motor #18-82098, Missouri license # 522-418...seized and held Fahey to travel to Minneapolis, Hennepin County, Minnesota, for purpose of preventing him from reporting unlawful seizure of said automobile to law enforcement and police officials and authorities for purpose of thus avoiding their apprehension and arrest...particularly to a point one and one half miles south of Champlin, Hennepin County, Minnesota.

•••

Meredith's wife, Vera, travels to Grand Rapids to visit him early Tuesday afternoon, accompanied by her brother, Roy Rootes, his wife Doris, and Deputy Harry Lamson. She has been called to Jack's bedside because attending physicians fear that Meredith will die.

Vera mourns the fate of her husband, of whom she says, "I still love, in spite of the fact that I have not seen him for two years and that he has meanwhile entered a life of crime."

However, after visiting Jack at the Grand Rapids Hospital, Vera states, "I don't think I love him anymore."

"You see, we haven't lived together for two years. I never saw him and only heard from him once or twice until he came to the farm."

Roy Rootes, Vera Meredith, Doris Rootes

When asked if she had talked to her husband, she does not reply.

Vera recalls how she met Meredith, four and a half years ago while she was still a schoolgirl and he was employed in a CCC camp at Deer Lake, near her father's farm.

Vera Marie Rootes and "John" Otis Meredith were married April 5, 1934 in Grand Rapids, Minnesota.

Their daughter, Deloris Marie Meredith, was born on January 2, 1935.

They lived for a while on her father's farm, they lived in Minneapolis for about a year, and then moved to St. Louis.

After they moved to St. Louis, they quarreled.

"I took the baby and came home. He had never seen her since then, that was June two years ago, until he came Sunday. Then he played with her and seemed to like her very much."

Vera and Deloris Meredith

According to Vera, Charles Rootes had heard a broadcast description of the kidnapping of Peggy Gross and Daniel Cox Fahey, Jr. in St. Louis.

When Vera's long absent husband drove up to the farm home early Sunday with a companion, Mr. Rootes became suspicious.

Meredith played with his 3 year-old daughter, Deloris Marie, and then went fishing. Mr. Rootes notified the officers of the CCC camp of his suspicions and they contacted the FBI.

As to the FBI raid, Vera states, "I saw it all. But I can't tell you what I did or what I said. I screamed and cried, I know."

•••

Mrs. Grace O'Neal, Meredith's mother, contacts the St. Louis office of the FBI stating that she has received a letter addressed to Jack Meredith, from Crowley's Ridge State Park in Walcott, Arkansas, advising that a fold containing several papers had been found by concessionaire W. R. Heagler on August 8th, and that the fold was being sent to the St. Louis Police Department, where Meredith could obtain possession of it upon identification.

At the St. Louis Police Department, FBI agents interviewed Lt. Joseph Lesyna, who acknowledged that he had received the fold from W. R. Heagler, which was believed to be the property of Otis James Meredith.

Examination of the fold revealed the following:
- Missouri drivers license # 233702 issued to Jack Meredith, 5912 DeGiverville, St. Louis, on March 9, 1937
- Missouri drivers license # 873194 issued to Jack Meredith
- Minnesota drivers license, dated January 30, 1936 at St. Paul
- Missouri automobile certificate to a 1935 Ford Tudor, Motor # 18-1653961
- 1936 Minnesota fishing license, issued to Jack Meredith of 2801 Portland, Minneapolis
- 1937 Missouri fishing license

•••

FBI Director Hoover sends a telegram to SAC Hendon in St. Paul:

PLEASE EXPRESS TO SPECIAL AGENTS HARDY AND NOONAN MY APPRECIATION AND COMMENDATION FOR THE VERY GOOD WORK WHICH THEY DID IN EFFECTING THE APPREHENSION OF JOHN COUCH AND OTIS JAMES MEREDITH.

•••

FBI agents in Memphis, Tennessee, shoot and kill Fred A. Tuttle after he opens fire on them.

The agents were investigating a tip that Tuttle might actually be Floyd Hamilton.

It turns out that Tuttle was wanted in several states for crimes ranging from bigamy to grand larceny.

•••

4:45 p.m.

Agent Noonan again visits Meredith, who states, "I'm glad you're back. They tried to kill me a while ago."

Jack was referring to the dressing of his wounds and the examination of his operation.

Meredith says that his wife had been in to see him. He asks that a wire be sent to his mother. Agent Noonan instructs Dr. McLeod to wire Meredith's mother and let her know that his condition is critical and that recovery was unlikely.

Noonan tells Meredith that he is in serious condition, but that he is tough.

Meredith replies, "I'm not tough. Did that girl in Minneapolis (Peggy) say I was?"

Noonan asks why they, "hit the man."

Meredith replies, "I only hit him because he tried to drive off. He pulled a dumb trick with two of us on the running board and two guns on him."

(Author's note: it was actually Couch who hit Fahey in the head with the butt of a gun).

Meredith continues, "I pulled a dumb trick last night. I shouldn't have ran but that was the first thing that entered my head."

Meredith asks Noonan, "How much do you think I'll get? I want to avoid the state rap and take the federal rap."

Meredith is very vague at this time, and it is difficult to obtain information from him.

Noonan asks him about the state charges, and Meredith replies that he had served two, one in the State Penitentiary in Jefferson City, and the other in the Missouri State Reformatory in Boonville. However, he didn't think they knew about both as he went to the Reformatory and then to the State Penitentiary and then back to the Reformatory and that there were two separate charges.

Noonan asks him if there were any state rap for which he is now wanted.

Meredith replies that there was a bank job, but with half a smile says that, "Hamilton and Walters are supposed to have pulled that."

After this statement, Meredith falls asleep for several hours.

•••

5:00 P.M.

SAC Norris in St. Louis sends a telegram to SAC Hendon in St. Paul:

MOTHER OTIS DESIRES KNOWLEDGE CONDITION OTIS AND IF SHE WOULD BE PERMITTED SEE HIM IN GRAND RAPIDS. ADVISE TELEGRAPHICALLY.

•••

5:05 p.m.

Couch makes his first statement to the FBI, in the Itasca County Jail:

STATEMENT OF JOHN COUCH

> *Grand Rapids, Minn.*
> *Aug. 16, 1938*
> *5:05 PM*

I, JOHN COUCH, give the following statement voluntarily to S. W. Hardy, Special Agent, Federal Bureau of Investigation, without threat or promise, in the presence of Deputy Sheriffs Harry Lamson, John Doyle and Otto Litchke of Itasca County, Minnesota, knowing that I do not have to make any statement and that this statement will be used against me in a prosecution.

About 2:00 A.M., Saturday morning, August 13, 1938, James Otis Meredeith and I kidnaped Daniel C. Fahey and Miss "Peggy" Gross of Warson Road in Clayton, Missouri. Miss Gross told us the point where we kidnapped them was about half a mile from her home.

At the time Meredeith and I came upon Fahey and Miss Gross, they were sitting and talking in the front seat of Mr. Fahey's Ford car, which was tan in color, was a Sedan with Motorola Radio, and carried Missouri license plates. This was the same Ford car which Meredeith and I had in our possession at Chas. Rootes home, 9 miles east of Effie, Minn., about 9:20 PM, August 15, 1938, when Meredeith and I were arrested by Federal Officers. We had not changed the Missouri license plates on the car.

At the time Meredeith and I came up to Fahey and Miss Gross at Clayton, Missouri. Meredeith and I each had pistols in our hands, these being the same two pistols which were in our possession at the time of our arrest Aug. 15, 1938. We stepped on the left running board of Fahey's car. Fahey started his car, but we made him stop the car. I told them to get out of the car and into the back seat. Fahey said to me, "Throw down that gun, and I'll whip you."

I did not hit Fahey, but when he got out of the car I shoved him against the car door and he hit his nose on the car and it started bleeding. Then Fahey and Miss Gross got in the rear seat, as I commanded them to do. Both Meredeith and I took turns driving the car, and we forced Fahey and Miss Gross to go with us, against their will. We drove in Fahey's car from Clayton, Missouri, to a point several miles north of Minneapolis, Minnesota, where Meredeith and I tied their hands and feet with baling wire or picture wire, which I bought in a hardware store in Southern Minnesota. I do not recall the town where I bought it. But we left Fahey and Miss Gross tied up in a field about 10:00 P.M., Aug. 13, 1938. On this trip we took Fahey and Miss Gross through Missouri, Iowa, Wisconsin, and Minnesota. The reason we kidnapped Fahey and Miss Gross was so we could have a car in which to come to Minnesota. The reason we did not let them go before we reached Minneapolis was because they could have notified the Police right away to look out for us and for the car.

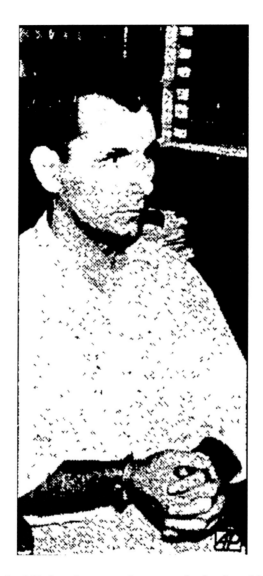

I asked Fahey how much money he had and he handed me his pocketbook and I looked in it and saw he had $2.00 in it, so I handed it back to him. Meredieth and I fed Fahey and Miss Gross sandwiches and milk at different places between Clayton, Missouri, and Minneapolis, Minnesota. We both tied Fahey and Miss Gross up.

After leaving Fahey and Miss Gross tied up, Meredeith and I drove Fahey's car to the Chas. Rootes home near Effie, Minn., so he could see his wife. We were at Rootes home on the night of Aug. 15, 1938, when officers came on us, and told us to put our hands up, that we were under arrest, that they were Federal Officers. Meredeith and I each had a pistol. Meredeith resisted arrest and ran.

About two weeks ago Meredeith and I were in an A model Green Ford car with Missouri license, which car Meredeith said belonged to him. We drove this car from St. Louis, Missouri, to a point between Dallas and Forth Worth, Texas, where officers shot at us and we shot at the officers. We abandoned this car and got away from the officers, but they caught two girl hitchhikers that we had picked up. I do not know where the pistols which Meredeith and I had on us at the time of our arrest Aug. 15, came from, but we were both using them.

On June 16, 1938, I was released on parole from the Missouri State Prison at Jefferson City, Missouri, from a 9-year sentence for car theft. I am on parole until 1942 for this.

I have read this statement and it is true. I sign each page voluntarily.

(s) JOHN COUCH

Witnesses:

S. W. Hardy, Sp. Agt. F.B.I., St. Paul, Minn.
Harry N. Lamson, Deputy Sheriff, Effie, Minn.
Otto Litchke, Deputy Sheriff, Grand Rapids, Minn.
John Doyle, Deputy Sheriff, Bovey, Minn.

•••

6:00 P.M.
  Special Agent in Charge Hendon sends a telegram to
SAC G. B. Norris of St. Louis, Missouri:

*MEREDITH CONDITION CRITICAL. CHANCES FOR
RECOVERY FIFTY FIFTY. MAY LAG ON SEVERAL DAYS.
NO OBJECTION HIS MOTHER SEEING HIM.*

•••

  Dr. McLeod reports to the FBI that he has been called
repeatedly by newspaper representatives, particularly by
reporter Smalley of the St. Paul Dispatch, who want to get into
the hospital to take a picture of Meredith.
  Dr. McLeod states that he told them all, and Smalley in
particular, that such procedure would be against the rules of the
hospital, that it would also be against his own rules, that he had
been instructed by agents not to permit the taking of any
pictures, and that regardless of all these reasons, he wouldn't
let the photographers in to take pictures anyway.
  Dr. McLeod says that reporter Smalley of the St. Paul
Dispatch was quite indignant and at the time of this refusal
attempted to get the number of the room occupied by Meredith,
but he refused to give it to him.
  Due to an attempt by photographers from the Duluth
newspaper to enter the hospital, Miss Mabel Korsell,
Superintendent of the hospital, has ordered the front door
watched and has ordered it fastened with a bolt and chain
during the evening and night. The agents noted that on several
occasions when entering and leaving the hospital, it was
necessary for the nurse on duty on the first floor to remove the
chain and bolt.

Representatives of the Duluth newspaper threaten to go over the head of Superintendent Korsell in an effort to get into the hospital for the purpose of taking pictures.

•••

7:06 p.m.

Fahey's car is transported to Gildemeister Motor Company in Grand Rapids for storage. They place its value at around $400.

Agent Noonan goes to Gildemeister's and makes the following notes: Tan 1935 Ford V8 Sedan, wire red wheels, red stripe around body, spare tire on rear, 57,580 miles, Missouri 1938 license 522-418, motor No. 18-82098. The glove compartment contained a St. Louis Street Guide, and a traffic booklet of the City of St. Louis.

Agent Noonan with Fahey's Car

He also found maps of Missouri, Virginia and Maryland, and another of the Northeastern United States.

Noonan found two bloody handkerchiefs in the back of the rear seat. These were probably from when Fahey got hit on the nose.

He also found a pair of pliers on the floor in front of the rear seat and a piece of wire on the back seat, similar to that with which the victims were tied.

•••

FBI Agents maintain a guard on Meredith's room at all times. No one is permitted to enter, other than the doctors and nurses at the hospital.

In order to get Meredith's fingerprints, the services of two agents are required. This is not done during the day to avoid any possible observation by other patients and visitors at the hospital, and because of the frequent calls made by doctors and nurses. It is determined that a good time to take Meredith's fingerprints would be about 8:00 p.m., before one agent left for the night.

At about 7:45 p.m., Dr. J. L. McLeod advises that the fingerprinting could be taken at any time without impairing Meredith's condition. Meredith is told that his fingerprints are wanted and he says that he will cooperate as best he can.

At approximately 8:00 p.m., Miss Mattson, the Night Nurse in Charge, is told that it is desired to get the fingerprints of Meredith.

Agents Notesteen and Noonan enter Meredith's room shortly after 8:00 p.m., and close the door, which has no lock on it. They take the fingerprints of Meredith's right hand. Nurse Watson enters the room to take Meredith's temperature, closing the door behind her. The agents move to the far side of the bed to take the fingerprints of Meredith's left hand.

168

Suddenly, the door is pushed open by reporter Smalley from the St. Paul Dispatch and flash photographs are taken. Smalley and his partner quickly exit down the corridor of the hospital, which is dark at the time.

St. Paul Dispatch Photo

The only way in which these men could have entered the hospital was through the self-operating elevator in the rear, in which patients are brought into the hospital on stretchers. Smalley had previously pushed open the doors on two rooms wherein there were maternity cases before locating Meredith's room. The nurse on duty said that the men assumed the attitude of visitors.

August 17, 1938

Wednesday

    The St. Paul Dispatch runs a front page photo of Meredith being fingerprinted in the hospital, with an accompanying story with the byline of "A Staff Writer."
    As a result of the newspapermen bursting into Meredith's hospital room the night before, a restraining order is requested of the Itasca County Attorney prohibiting all newspaper photographers from entering the hospital.

•••

    John Couch is transported by Special Agent Hardy and Itasca County Sheriff Elmer Madson from Grand Rapids, Minnesota, to St. Paul, Minnesota, where he is arraigned before US Commissioner W. T. Goddard at about 2:00 p.m.
    Couch is manacled to a federal agent as he waives his preliminary hearing.

When Goddard asks Couch if he desires an attorney, John replies, "No sir, I made the confession. I pleaded guilty."

The guilty plea cannot be accepted as final, however, since an indictment is necessary on such a major charge.

Bail is set at $100,000 on each of the two charges, and Couch is led away to the Ramsey County Jail, at St. Peter and Fourth Street in St. Paul, by Deputy US Marshal Joseph Wessel, assisted by SAC Hendon, SA Hardy, and Sheriff Madson. He will be held until the next term of the Federal Grand Jury, which has been called for September 20, 1938.

•••

SA Noonan contacts Mr. Storey, manager of Roxy Studio in Grand Rapids, to take photographs of Meredith in the hospital to show to Fahey and Miss Gross for further identification.

•••

Dr. J. L. McLeod states late Wednesday that he doubts Meredith will live. Later, however, Jack shows some signs of improvement.

August 18, 1938

Thursday

Meredith's condition continues to improve, but he is still in serious condition.

•••

12:15 a.m.

Special Agent Noonan talks again with Meredith intermittently until about 12:45 a.m. Meredith is very lucid at times.

Noonan tells Meredith about what Peggy Gross had said, about him telling her to tell police not to shoot him in the head. Meredith smiles and tries to reach over to pat Noonan on the shoulder and says, "That's right, I always treated people OK. I never did go for that rough stuff."

Meredith says that he told Peggy that he would write to her, and admits that he asked her and Fahey to team up with him and Couch in a criminal career.

Noonan tells Meredith that if he, "went out," that he should, "go out clear." He says that since Meredith had said that he had never killed anybody, that he should give him information that would clear things up, and that he should do it before his Mother arrives.

Meredith tells Noonan that he and Couch had a couple of bad breaks, and several times mentions that he has something to tell him, but that he should not to be in a hurry.

A while into their conversation, Meredith says, "I will tell you now. One of those bad breaks was a botched bank robbery."

Noonan asks him about the bank job, to which Meredith replies, "Clearwater, Texas, and this was just a short time ago." Noonan asks him about the exact date, to which Meredith asks what date he was arrested.

Meredith is confused about when the alleged bank robbery occurred, except to say it was in the past two or three weeks. "We didn't get anything. They chased us off."

Noonan asks him about the other bad break.

Meredith says, "A woman ran off on us." He then describes in piecemeal that they held up a dance hall or tavern, and the wife of the owner or manager had moved or hidden the money, or something of the sort. He says that they could not wait because the Highway Patrol Headquarters was only a few miles down the road and he said that the patrol was after them.

"We took the place all right, and got quite a lot of small change, but missed the big money." He does not recall the name of the town, but says it is about 35 miles southeast of Kansas City.

He goes on to say that there were so many places that they had taken that he cannot recall many of them definitely. He says that he started his criminal career about 1928 or 1929.

He says that when he went to the penitentiary his reform school sentence was not mentioned in court, but that he had been fingerprinted in both places and both charges were probably known to authorities. If not, he does not want that to get out.

Jack goes on to relate how he, Couch and James Clyde Reed were in on the bank job in Clearwater, Texas, and the dance hall job, and several others. He says that Reed was a boozer and got drunk and got caught just before they left for Minnesota. (It should be noted that Reed barely made it out of Missouri with Couch and Meredith, and was never in Texas with them).

Meredith goes on, "These guys always go for cracking people over the head with their guns to knock them out, but I didn't go for that, and had arguments with them about it."

Meredith refers to the information he has just given Noonan and asks, "You won't let that out, will you, because it will make it tough on me when I get to the Pen if they knew I told you?"

Meredith states, regarding his wounds and the shooting, "I don't blame anyone. I should not have run. There was nothing they could do but stop me, and I probably would have gotten away if I had just gotten around that shed."

He says that the buckshot hitting him knocked him down, then he felt the revolver bullet immediately after.

"This is a losing game. I got only what I should have expected."

Meredith states that he had no money other than five dollars and some change, which was found on him when he was arrested. He says that he has not hidden any money, and if he had, he would not tell Noonan about it. He again states that they had some bad breaks, and had not taken much money.

Noonan asks Meredith about a statement Couch had made about the Minnesota Highway Patrol attempting to stop them, to which Meredith replies that nothing like that happened in Minnesota, but that it was the Highway Patrol in Texas. "They don't have what it takes, but you can't blame them."

Meredith then fades into sleep.

•••

Early in the morning, Hoover fires off a reply to a memo he received a few days earlier from Mr. Gordon Dean:

Memorandum to Mr. Gordon Dean, Special Executive Assistant to the Attorney General
From J. Edgar Hoover, Director of the FBI

Upon my return to the city I received your memorandum of August 16, 1938, concerning the memorandum which was forwarded to you on that date by the Bureau dealing with the capture of Otis James Meredith and John Couch.

Before dealing with some of the details of this matter, I do want to express my resentment at the statement which you make to the effect that the procedure followed in this case was "contrary to the clear understanding which we reached with the Attorney General on this subject some months ago." In the first place, this is not correct, and in the second place I am not cognizant of the existence at the present time of any Departmental order which gives you the right or authority to censure me for acts of administration of this Bureau. If my understanding of the Departmental set-up is correct, such action as that at the present time, at least, is reserved to the Attorney General and to the Assistant to the Attorney General. When I have misconstrued or misinterpreted any orders of the Attorney General, I stand ready to receive censure from him or from the Assistant Attorney General, and from no one else.

In regard to the details of this matter and to my statement that you conclude that I have violated an understanding which I had with the Attorney General is not one of fact, I predicate that statement of mine on the ground that the case in question was not a national case. In the first place, while technically the actions of Meredith and Couch constituted a violation of the Federal Kidnaping Statute, there was not involved in this case any aspect of ransom nor any aspect of a national character. These two criminals had taken a man and a woman from St. Louis to Minnesota and there had left them by the side of a road. It was obvious their purpose was to steal an automobile rather than to take two persons for ransom. Technically, however, there was a violation of the Federal Kidnaping Statute. There have been many cases of this kind, none of which has ever been the subject of a Washington release, because they have been but technical violations of the Federal Kidnaping Statutes, and the releases thereon have emanated from the local field office of the Bureau.

For your information, the arrests of Meredith and Couch were effected at 9:00 p.m. on August 15th, and in effecting the arrests some shooting took place with the resultant injury to Meredith. He reached the hospital about midnight on August 15th. Had it been a case of national scope I doubt whether it would have been possible to have gotten a release out of Washington upon the matter, because, quite frankly, I have given up endeavoring to contact you after 5:00 or 5:30 p.m. In so many instances when I have endeavored to reach you at your home either there was no answer or I could not ascertain where you were in order to make such releases as might have considered desirable.

Reverting to the Meredith and Couch case, obviously when there has been an arrest made in which there was a shooting, and in which it is necessary to remove a person seriously wounded to a hospital, and when the arrests were made with the assistance of local authorities, it is impossible - whether it is your desire or mine – to withhold information concerning such a case until the convenience of Washington can be served for the purpose of making a release. The initial steps in this apprehension, as has been previously pointed out, occurred at 9:00 p.m. on August 15th. I was in constant telephonic touch with my St. Paul office and I was advised by it about 5:00 or 6:00 a.m., on the morning of August 16th. That they were receiving innumerable inquiries by the press in St. Paul, inquiring as to what it was all about. I authorized the St. Paul office to briefly set forth what the facts were. This was done. It was purely a local case and the only reason that the Washington papers gave any attention to it was because one of the victims happened to be a Washington man. He did not appear in the headlines or on the front page of any other newspaper in any other part of the country other than in St. Paul, St. Louis, and Washington D.C. The proposed release which was forwarded to your office was sent by me due to the fact that this case had a Washington angle to it.

For your further information, several times during the morning of August 16th I personally from New York inquired from my office whether you could be reached in your office so that I could discuss the making of a release from Washington, and inquiries there brought the response that you were not in. I was not certain whether a release should in fact be prepared for Washington consumption, and I had wanted to talk with you about that, but I was unable to reach you on the morning of August 16th. I finally instructed Mr. Foxworth, who was acting in my absence, to prepare a memorandum and to send it around to you just as soon as it was ascertained that you had arrived at the office, and that was at 10:06 a.m. on the morning of August 16th. As I have indicated, it was not sent with the idea that it was a national release, but in order to enable you to answer any inquiries which might be made by the Washington papers. You would have had this information considerably sooner had it been possible for me to reach you by telephone.

There was no formal release prepared at St. Paul by the St. Paul office, and they merely stated what had occurred. To have refrained from answering those inquiries at St. Paul would have undoubtedly resulted in a hostile attitude upon the part of the newspapers in that area, which had already learned of the arrest, and of the fact that a wounded man was in the hospital, and which had already contacted the local sheriff who had aided us in effecting the arrest. It would have been silly and absurd for our Agent in Charge at St. Paul to have remained mute and have referred all inquiries to you in Washington. We are dealing with very practical matters in this Bureau, and it is imperative that the good will of the press be maintained.

We can't maintain that with a lot of restrictions that serve no really useful purpose.

Probably I will receive from you in the course of the next twenty four hours some protest relative to the releasing of information in Memphis, Tennessee concerning the killing of Frederick A. Tuttle, a notorious criminal who in a gun battle with our Agents wounded one of the Agents of this Bureau. In this particular matter, the shooting occurred at approximately 4:30 p.m. August 16th. Again at 5:00 or 5:30 p.m., when I took charge of the matter by long distance from New York, I knew that it was useless to try to get a release out of Washington. In addition thereto, the press of Memphis were vigorously demanding information from our Agent in Charge at Memphis. For him to have stalled and to have waited until some formal release could have been prepared would have resulted in a most critical attitude upon the part of the Memphis press toward this Bureau. I subsequently told the Agent in Charge at Memphis that he might give the press the basic facts of the shooting and the reasons for trying to effect the arrest of the man who had to be killed. This he did.

In order that there be no resentment or criticism upon the part of departmental officials, I declined to make any statement to the press at New York, though I was solicited by a quite a number with the result that a number of them indicated that they thought if was rather high-handed bureaucracy for me not even to make a comment concerning the shooting of one of the Agents of this Bureau. I feared if I did that, the mere appearance of my name in some newspaper dispatch would cause additional irritation upon the part of some person, so I remained silent and allowed the Agent in Charge at Memphis to briefly tell what the facts were. Again, it was not a case of national importance and again it was not carried in the headlines of any newspapers other than those in the area of Memphis, Tennessee, so, consequently, I thought that irrespective of whether it would have been physically possible to get a release out of Washington, it was not a case which warranted a release from Washington.

Very truly yours,
John Edgar Hoover
Director

•••

3:00 p.m.

Meredith's mother Grace arrives at the hospital with his sister Geraldine, and one of his brothers, Alfred. She tells Noonan that she has told the St. Louis Office all that she knows about the case and had given them what cooperation she could.

She speaks highly of her treatment by the St. Louis FBI Office, but bitterly against her treatment by St. Louis Police.

She tells Noonan that Meredith had left her home about a month earlier, and she has not seen him since. Prior to that he had been living with her and seldom went out at night. He brought Couch to her home once and she did not like his looks or his actions. She told Otis not to bring him there again. She says that she told Otis that she could not pick his company, but could say whom he should or could bring to her home. Otis had told her about a week before he left home that he and Couch had split up.

•••

Deputy US Marshal Earnest Drew takes over custody of Meredith from the FBI at the hospital and reads him the two kidnapping warrants against him.

•••

A diagram of the scene of the shooting is prepared by Agent Noonan and is forwarded to the FBI Bureaus in St. Paul and Washington.

•••

4:25 p.m.

SAC Hendon in St. Paul calls Washington regarding the case. It appears that Meredith may recover. His mental state is normal at this time, and if he lives, it will be possible to move him in two or three weeks. The FBI has turned guard and custody of Meredith over to US Marshals. The agents have talked to Meredith quite a bit, but there is still a great deal of interviewing to take place.

Meredith has inferred that he, Couch and Reed may have attempted to rob a bank at Clearwater, Texas, recently, and that he also robbed some dance hall or tavern outside of Kansas City.

August 19, 1938

Friday

Meredith dies suddenly at 12:40 a.m.

He had rallied Wednesday night and on Thursday was believed to be on the road to recovery.

Dr. McLeod calls Meredith's mother into the hospital. He then takes her to meet Wes Libbey, who is the County Coroner as well as an undertaker, who handles the arrangements. Mrs. O'Neal pays the charges, and selects a casket for $375, and arranges for the immediate removal of the body to Ashdown, Arkansas.

The family heads back to St. Louis, and Meredith's body leaves Coleraine, Minnesota, by train at noon. Mrs. O'Neal requests that no information be released about the time or place of the removal.

Dr. McLeod signs the death certificate.

Under "Cause of death," he notes, "Homicide in Carpenter Township, Itasca County, shot by Federal Agents." In the part of the certificate pertaining to surgery, McLeod simply puts that, "Surgery was performed to repair abdomen." No mention is made of the specific wounds, as reporters had been hounding the hospital trying to get detailed information about the wounds. Dr. McLeod states that he will keep the X-rays in his file, and they can be produced at any time needed by the authorities.

•••

Gladys Rootes, her son Roy Rootes, and his wife Doris Rootes give statements to Special Agent S. W. Hardy.

They state that Vera married Meredith in 1934 when he was working at the CCC Camp near Effie. They did not know he was an ex-convict until he told them after they were married.

Vera returned to Effie from St. Louis around September 1, 1936.

Meredith did not send support for his wife or child, and there is an active warrant against him in Itasca County.

Meredith had not written to his wife since May 1937, except for a letter sent in May 1938, in which he wrote her asking for a divorce.

When the Rootes' woke up Sunday morning August 14th, there was a tan Ford with Missouri license plates parked near their home. Mr. and Mrs. Roy Rootes walked out to the car and found Meredith and Couch. Couch was introduced as Johnny.

Couch and Meredith stayed at the Rootes house August 14th and 15th. Couch told Roy Rootes that he owned the Ford and that he still owed $125 on it. Jack said that they drove up to visit Vera because Couch had a vacation from his job in St. Louis. They had no baggage with them.

Around 11:00 a.m. Sunday, August 14th, Meredith drove members of the Rootes family to visit the Grahams in Bigfork, Minnesota. Couch stayed behind at the Rootes farm and sat out in the underbrush about 200 feet from the house until Meredith returned.

In the afternoon on Sunday, Roy Rootes, Mrs. Roy Rootes, Lloyd Rootes (age 13), and Luther Rootes (age 15), went fishing with Couch and Meredith. During this trip Couch and Meredith shot at road signs and other targets with their pistols.

Monday, when Couch and Meredith drove to Effie with Carl Rootes and Lloyd Rootes, they again shot at road signs with their pistols.

The Rootes' went on to describe what happened when the officers arrived at their home around 9:20 p.m. the evening of the 15th.

August 20, 1938

Saturday

In US District Court in St. Louis, Ruth Baker and Hattie May Stevens waive removal to Dallas.

August 21, 1938

Sunday

Floyd Hamilton was captured afoot and unarmed by two Dallas detectives early today, shortly after he had escaped from federal agents.

A few hours before, his companion in crime, Huron Ted Walters, had been picked up in downtown Dallas, ending a nationwide manhunt for the FBI's #1 and #2 "Most Wanted."

Police said the two men had lived for several days in a hideout in Dallas with 30 year-old Willie Marshall, who was arrested on suspicion of harboring fugitives from justice. Marshall met the two men on a freight train when they were heading towards Dallas from Texarkana.

Police first got word of the presence of the desperadoes in Dallas when they saw Marshall carrying messages to Hamilton's friends and family.

Willie Marshall was supposedly arrested, grilled, and was reported to have given information to the FBI which led them to the hideout.

Walters had gone to the home of his cousin, Elmer Walls, Saturday night. When he met two men with shotguns upon entering the home, he knew that he had made a mistake. Instead of running, he walked right on in.

"I'm one of the Walls boys," he announced.

Walters then went upstairs and put on one of his cousin's shirts. He brewed some coffee and drank it. Then he went back downstairs, picked up a guitar and played some music.

About 1:30 a.m. Sunday, Hamilton arrived at the house. The federal agents opened the door and invited him in.

"I haven't got time," Hamilton shouted, and started to run.

One of the officers started after him, firing a shotgun. Hamilton was wounded in the leg, but kept on running.

J. W. Cox, who was sleeping in the yard of his home nearby, was awakened by the shooting and started running too.

The agent got the two men mixed up and started chasing Cox. Mrs. Lucille Cox, who saw the excitement, said that Walters ran out on the porch and started jumping up and down and screaming at the top of his lungs. "He was acting so crazy the Federal Officers asked him if he was drunk."

A half hour later, Walters sneaked out the back of the house, while the officers stood watch at the front door waiting for Huron Ted Walters to arrive.

Walters then walked into a group of Dallas Policemen about three blocks away and was arrested.

Hamilton was limping along the Trinity River bottom toward a railroad track, attempting to catch a freight train out of town, when Detectives Will Fritz and Jack Archer of the Dallas Police Department found him.

Hamilton surrendered without a fight. He had several buckshot wounds in his left leg, which was badly inflamed.

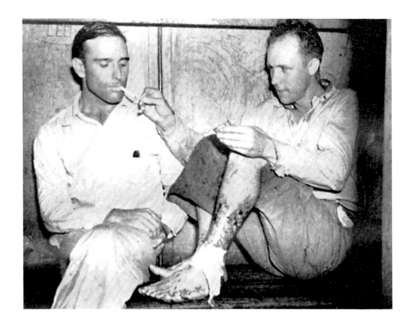

Huron Ted Walters and Floyd Hamilton

Neither Hamilton nor Walters were armed, and both were dirty and unkempt.

Walters, who broke into the limelight for the first time when he escaped with Floyd from jail in Montague, Texas, denied that he and Hamilton had pulled any big jobs and pointed to his ragged appearance as proof.

He admitted that he and Hamilton had been in the woods between DeQueen, Arkansas, and Broken Bow, Oklahoma, for two weeks where federal, state and local officers were searching for them.

"We saw the officers and their bloodhounds lots of time," Walters said.

"We hid out in that country for about ten days. I swam some river up there five times in order to keep from being captured. It was up there that we lost our guns.

"Finally we got a chance to get into Texarkana and caught a freight train to Dallas."

Huron Ted Walters stated that, "Fifty percent of the robberies and highjackings attributed to us were committed by others."

Hamilton denied participating in the machine gun robbery of a Wood River, Illinois, bank messenger August 6th, when $34,000 was taken.

"I wish I had," Hamilton said when questioned about the robbery.

Hamilton, who had only $6.24 and two handfuls of .45 caliber pistol cartridges in his pocket, said he never owned a machine gun, but added, "I bought one, but was never able to pick it up."

Walters, who had no money on him when police picked him up, said Dallas police credited him with about 14 robberies, but that he and Hamilton had nothing to do with thirteen of them.

August 23, 1938

Tuesday

Itasca County Hospital submits a bill for services rendered to James Otis Meredith in the amount of $57.00.

•••

A funeral for James Otis Meredith is held in Ashdown, Arkansas, where he is buried in his Grandparent's family plots in Hudson Cemetery

Funeral for Meredith Held at Ashdown, Ark.

ASHDOWN, Ark., Aug. 23.--(AP)--Funeral services for Otis Meredith, 21, alleged kidnaper slain by officers at Grand Rapids, Minn., last Friday, were held here today.

The service was attended by Meredith's aunt and uncle who live near here; his mother, Mrs. Grace O'Neil of St. Louis, and other relatives,

August 24, 1938

Wednesday

SAC Hendon in St. Paul sends a message to the Washington FBI Office:

Excellent cooperation was received in this case from Dr. James H. Bender, Bigfork, Minnesota, who attended Meredith immediately after the shooting in Bigfork, and accompanied the agents to the Itasca Hospital in Grand Rapids, Minnesota; from Dr. J. Lawrence McLeod, Marr Building, Grand Rapids, Minnesota, who is a State Senator, and attended Meredith with Dr. Bender up until his death, and who signed his death certificate; and from Miss Mabel Korsell, Superintendent of the Itasca County Hospital, Grand Rapids.

It is suggested that letters of appreciation be sent to these individuals by the director. It is further suggested in the letter to Miss Korsell, that appreciation be expressed through her to all of the hospital employees. Their assistance in every way was exceptional.

...

John Couch gives his second statement to the FBI:

SECOND STATEMENT OF DEFENDANT:

This statement was taken August 24, 1938, at the Ramsey County Jail, St. Paul, Minnesota by Special Agent S.W. Hardy:

I, JOHN COUCH, give the following statement voluntarily without threat or promise from any source, to S.W. Hardy, Special Agent of the Federal Bureau of Investigation. I know that I do not have to make any statement, and I know that this statement will be used against me in a prosecution. I met James Otis Meredeith and James C. Reed while all three of us were serving sentences in the Boonville, Missouri Reformatory in 1932. Reed was also in Jefferson City, Missouri, Prison with me from 1933 to 1937. I was released from Jefferson City, Missouri Prison on parole June 16, 1938, and will be on parole until 1942. About July 19, 1938, I met MEREDEITH in a beer tavern in St. Louis, Mo. Two nights later I went back to this same tavern with my brother, Russell, and saw MEREDEITH again. MEREDEITH asked me if I had a job yet, and I told him "No." MEREDEITH said, "Maybe you and I can get together again and make a little money. I am not working either." I asked him "Well, how do you mean we can make a little money". MEREDEITH told me that we could cruise around and look over a place, and that if it satisfied me we will go in and take a couple of drinks, and then if it looks all right to you and you think we can take it alone, you can do that, and I will wait for you down the road a couple of blocks and pick you up after you have taken it." Russell Couch overheard this and he told MEREDEITH that I had just gotten out of prison, and he would not like to see me do anything to get into trouble again, and he advised MEREDEITH and me not to do anything like that. So then Russell told MEREDEITH about "my brother George who is serving life sentence in Missouri Prison for murder of a policeman, and I helped put George in prison, and I am sorry I did it." Then Russell told MEREDEITH that he was trying to help me in every way he could to keep me out of prison. Then MEREDEITH walked away, and motioned for me to come over to his table where he was sitting. I went over to MEREDEITH and he said, "If you take your brother home, and come back, I will tell you something worth your time". I told MEREDEITH I would see him next Sunday night at this same tavern, which was on Taylor and Page Avenue in St. Louis, Mo.

I met MEREDEITH there the next Sunday night. He took me out to a Ford sedan car, which he had outside, and he showed me a .38 caliber Smith and Wesson blue steel revolver. MEREDEITH said "I have had a few words with my mother, and she is beginning to think that I am getting myself in trouble." He asked me if I wanted to leave town and if I knew of anyone who would want to go along. I told him we could go down to Reed's house on Evans Avenue in St. Louis – I think the number was 1914 or 1419, I am not sure of this number. When we got there I asked Reed if he wanted to leave St. Louis. Reed asked us where we were going. We told Reed that we did not have any particular place in mind where we wanted to go. So then I told MEREDEITH to explain to Reed what it was all about. So MEREDEITH told Reed that we were going on the road and when we ran short of money we could stop in somewhere and stick a place up, and get some money to travel on. Reed asked us if the car belonged to MEREDITH, or if it as a stolen car. MEREDEITH told Reed that the car belonged to him, that he had paid for it.

Reed said "all right, wait till I get some of my clothes together and some things I will need." We waited about 20 minutes and Reed came out and got in the car with us. The .38 caliber pistol was the only pistol we had at the time.

We started out from St. Louis, Mo., and MEREDEITH stopped off at St. Charles, Missouri, and he went into a place which was a house where MEREDEITH said a fellow lived who he had known for some time, and who he believed he could get a couple of pistols from. I don't know the name of the person or the address of the place where we stopped. MEREDEITH returned to the car with the same two .38 caliber pistols which were in my possession at the time we were arrested.

We three then drove from St. Charles, Mo. To Greenwood, Mo. I believe this was about July 31, 1938. About a mile or two outside of Greenwood MEREDEITH was driving and he ran the Ford off into the ditch and must have torn the rear end out, because we could not get it to pull itself out of the ditch. That is where I cut my nose when the car ran off into the ditch. We worked to try to get the car back on the road for about fifteen minutes, and we saw we could not get it back, so we took our baggage out of the car, took the license plates off, and set the car afire. While it was burning we saw another car coming down the highway and I stepped out in front of the car and tried to flag him down, but I saw the driver was not going to stop, so I got out of the way to keep from getting run over. I watched this car after it passed us, and saw it pull into the driveway about half a mile from where we were. This was around 1:00 a.m. I told MEREDEITH and Reed, "We are stranded here, and there is only one thing we can do - - and that is to go up there and take that fellow's car." MEREDEITH and Reed did not approve of the plan, and said, "Let's wait awhile for something else to come along." I told them, "If we wait around too long, some one will notice the flames from the car, and come along to investigate."

I said, "Well if you fellows won't help me, I will get the car by myself." I walked up the road, and just as I got to the place where I had seen the car turn in, the man driving the car was getting out of the car. His car was a black Buick sedan about a 1934 or 1935 model I believe, carrying Missouri license plates. I took hold of the man's belt from behind and stuck my pistol in his back and I said, "Don't get excited, I only want your automobile". I told him, "Just get in the back seat, and I won't harm you." He got in the back seat, and I got in behind the wheel, and drove down to where Reed and MEREDEITH were waiting for me at the burning car. This man told us that his name was Kalousek and that his father had been connected with the Sheriff's Office of that county.

MEREDEITH and Reed walked over to the car, and I told MEREDEITH, "You better take the wheel." Then I got in the back seat, and MEREDEITH drove the car. Reed got in the front seat. They put all the baggage in the Buick car. I asked Kalousek, "If your father has been Sheriff, you ought to be a pretty good shot yourself". He said, "I can shoot a gun". I let him shoot the .38 cal. Pistol once, but he knew that MEREDEITH and Reed had pistols trained on him at the time and that they would shoot him if he tried to shoot any of us. After letting him shoot the revolver once I took the gun back from Kalousek. We then drove to Boonville, Mo. in this stolen Buick, and on the way there, Kalousek asked us what we were going to do with him. So Reed and I told him we were going to tie him up where he could be found in the morning. Kalousek said, "Well if you are going to tie me up, get me some whiskey and soda, so I can go to sleep. It is just a couple of hours before daybreak." So Reed bought half a pint of whiskey and a bottle of soda at a drug store in Boonville, Mo. We gave Kalousek the whiskey and he drank about half of it, and all of the soda. Then we took Kalousek out by the rock quarry at

Boonville, Mo. where the inmates of the reformatory work, because we knew that he would be found there in the morning, because the inmates work there every morning. It is about three miles from the reformatory. We took Kalousek out of the car, walked him over to the grass at the side of the road, and then I tied him up with extension cord electric wire, tying his hands and feet. Reed and MEREDEITH stood by watching as I tied him up.

Reed, MEREDEITH and I then drove in this stolen Buick of Kalousek's to Kennett, Mo. We got gasoline there at some filling station on the highway, and then we were driving to Cape Girardeau, Mo. Reed saw two girls, Hattie Mae Stevens and Ruth Baker, hitchhikers, who were sitting on a little bridge over a creek. Reed said, "I believe there were two hitchhikers back there. Let's go back and ask them if they want to ride." We went back and asked them if they wanted a ride, and they accepted our invitation to ride. Up to that time we had no particular place in mind to go to, but we asked the girls where they were going and the Stevens girl said she wanted to go to Paragould, Arkansas, to visit her husband. So I told her, "Well we are going to Paragould, Arkansas. We were just pulling up at a stop sign in Paragould and an officer pulled up along side us, and asked us, "Where are you going?" I told MEREDEITH to "Drive on," and the girls were in the car with us when this happened. MEREDEITH drove on out of the town of Paragould, Ark. Then Reed decided he wanted to buy some more whiskey. MEREDEITH and I both told Reed, "If you buy any more whiskey we are going to drive off and leave you." Reed said, "You would not do that." I said, "All right you go in there to buy whiskey and you will find out if I don't keep my word to leave you." Reed went into the whiskey store several miles from Paragould, Arkansas, so while he was gone we gave his hat and his coat and $5 to the filling station attendant to give him when he came out of the liquor store; and MEREDEITH, I and Miss Stevens and Miss Baker drove on.

We went to Texarkana, Texas, and drove around there a while looking for a place to stay but could not find a place that looked safe enough for us. After leaving Texarkana we drove to Dallas, Texas, still in this Buick we had stolen from Kalousek at Greenwood, Mo.

I forgot to mention that at Paragould, Arkansas, MEREDEITH and I both had given $12 apiece to Reed, so that he could buy a 30-30 rifle, lever action, at some store there. When we got to Dallas, Texas, about August 6, 1938, in the evening, MEREDEITH and I had this 30-30 rifle, a double barrel shotgun which we had bought at a second hand store in Texarkana, the two .32 cal. Revolvers, and a .38 cal. Revolver in the car. About 8:30 p.m. on August 6, 1938 – I believe this is the correct date – MEREDEITH, I, Miss Stevens and Miss Baker in this stolen Buick pulled up to a barbeque stand on the outskirts of Dallas, Texas. I think this stand is on the highway which leads out of Dallas towards Fort Worth, Texas. Miss Baker and Miss Stevens danced a few dances, then came back to the car where MEREDEITH and I were. Miss Baker told me, "That fellow in the car behind you just motioned for me to come over there where he is." I looked around and saw the red lights on the car she meant, and I saw it was a police car. The red light had the word "stop" across the center of it. We told the girls to "Come on, get in the car and let's get out of here." So they got in, and MEREDEITH and I drove away. We drove about a half a mile down the road towards Fort Worth, and the highway patrolmen – two of them, in the first car – pulled up alongside our car, and one of them said to us, "Pull over there, you." I looked up into the rear vision mirror, and saw MEREDEITH was looking at me in the mirror, and I signaled to him to "give her the gas." MEREDEITH increased his speed, and the officers threw on their red stop light, and their siren started to sound. When they saw we were trying to get away the officers started shooting.

Their first shot missed, but their second shot came through the car. MEREDEITH hollered to me, "Don't let them get us John." I said, "I'll do the best I can." I shot with the .38 caliber pistol through the rear window; and emptied this pistol shooting at the officers' car. The officers kept gaining speed on me, so I picked up the shotgun and shot twice at the officers with it. I hit their windshield, and they pulled over to the side of the road and parked, but their were two other cars full of officers and they continued to chase us, but they were too far away to shoot at us, so right after we looked back and saw the other two cars full of officers go right on by without noticing that we had made the turn off the main highway. We drove through a farmer's yard, and we ran into a little ditch or a creek and the car stalled there. The girls and MEREDEITH and I jumped out of the car and ran into the woods. The girls ran one way and we ran another. MEREDEITH and I took all our guns, but we left our clothes in this same Buick which we had stolen from Kalousek at Greenwood, Mo. That was the last we saw of the girls. The girls should have known the car was stolen when we ran off from the officer at Paragould, Arkansas, and knew we had pistols on us.

After leaving the Buick, MEREDEITH and I walked in the woods until we came to a little river. MEREDEITH swam across, and told me to throw the guns across to him. I tried to throw the .38 caliber revolver to him but it was too far a throw and the gun fell into the water. MEREDEITH had one of the .32 caliber pistols. I had the other .32 cal. revolver and shotgun on me, and I swam the river with them. The bullets in the shotgun had gotten wet and would not shoot, so I threw the shotgun away, and only kept the .32 caliber revolver. MEREDEITH and I walked through the woods for two days until we reached Arlington, Texas; and there we saw an elderly gentleman who said his name was Davenport. He was sitting near the depot in Arlington, Texas, in a 1935 Ford sedan,

*which had Texas license plates on it. MEREDEITH and I
walked up to Mr. Davenport and I asked him "How far is it to
the next town". Davenport said, "What did you say". I told
him, "Get into the back seat". Davenport said, "What is this,
a stickup". I said, "No, we just want your automobile".
Davenport saw my revolver then, which I was carrying in my
hand, and he said, "Oh, all right", and he got into the back
seat. We drove him about fifty miles, and then released him.
That was in Texas, but I do not remember the name of the
town. We drove his car some five or ten miles beyond the place
where we had released Davenport; and something went wrong
with the car, it was stalled on us and we could not get it
started; so we left that Ford car standing there, and we went to
the woods. This was on August 8, 1938. We made our way to
a railroad and rode the boxcars into St. Louis, Missouri. When
we were coming into the freight yards at St. Louis, Missouri, a
railroad officer saw us, and called us to stop, but we ran, and
the officer fired one shot at us but did not hit us. This was on
Friday, August 12, when we arrived in St. Louis. We then went
to the home of my sister, Mrs. Frances Witter, in St. Louis.
When she saw me she told me that the St. Louis Police Officers
had been to her home looking for me, and for me not to come
in; as the police had told her that if they found me in her house
it would get her in a lot of trouble. And she said, "You know I
have four children here and I can not afford to get into any
trouble." So I told her "goodbye" and we left. MEREDEITH
and I each had a .32 cal. pistol on us at that time. This was
late Friday evening August 12, 1938. The two of us walked to
Warson Road in Clayton, Missouri, where we found Mr. Fahey
and Miss Gross in a Ford car, and we kidnaped them, and
forced them to go against their will from Clayton, Mo. to a
point north of Minneapolis in Minnesota where we tied them
up. The details of how MEREDEITH and I kidnapped Fahey*

*and Miss Gross have been given by me in a previous statement
and are true.*

I have read this statement and it is true and correct.

/s/   JOHN COUCH

Witnesses:

SAMUEL W. HARDY, Special Agent,
Federal Bureau of Inv.
St. Paul, Minnesota

EMORY J. CLEWETT
Deputy Sheriff,
St. Paul, Minnesota

August 25, 1938

Thursday

SAC Hendon sends the bill from Dr. J. H. Bender of the
Itasca Clinic in Bigfork, Minnesota, for services rendered to
Meredith, to US Marshal John J. Ferrell in St. Paul.
"It is my understanding that the prices charged by Dr.
Bender are those rates in effect in Itasca County," Hendon
States.

•••

Tom Neal and D. B. Davis, Federal Bureau of
Investigation agents in Dallas, resigned from the Service after
failing to capture Floyd Hamilton and Huron Ted Walters in a
trap early Sunday morning.

The agents occupied a house where the two outlaws were expected to take refuge. Walters came to the house and was not recognized, and Hamilton also appeared and escaped under gunfire.

August 26, 1938

Friday

SAC Hendon sends a letter to FBI Director Hoover in Washington concerning photographs taken by the St. Paul Dispatch under the date of August 17, 1938, purporting to be that of Otis James Meredith and two agents taken at the Itasca County Hospital, Grand Rapids, Minnesota. The agents that were photographed, but not easily identified, are Special Agents E. N. Notesteen and R. T. Noonan of the St. Paul Office.

September 1, 1938

Thursday

A memo is written by Harold Nathan, Assistant Director of Investigations of the FBI, in reference to the scandal caused by the St. Paul Dispatch in photographing Meredith in his hospital bed, that reads:

I think it would be a good idea if someone would collect some of these ghoulish evidence of modern journalism. I suppose this is the 'freedom of the press' which, if curtailed would mean the country's downfall.

There is a handwritten response on the typed memo which says, "I thoroughly agree," followed by an initial which looks like a stylized "A."

September 2, 1938

Friday

Ruth Baker and Hattie Bass are brought from St. Louis to Dallas, Texas, where they are arrested and held on a federal auto theft charge.

The two, said by officers to have been companions of Otis John Meredith and John Couch, will be tried in Federal Court either in Dallas or Fort Worth in November.

September 3, 1938

Saturday

Today is John Couch's 23rd birthday.

•••

Hoover replies to Hendon in regards to the St Paul Dispatch fiasco:

With reference made to your letter dated August 26, 1938, regarding the unethical activities of newspaper photographers in securing the photograph of Otis James Meredith being fingerprinted, it is desired that you forward to the Bureau at an early date a copy of the restraining order secured by the County Attorney at Grand Rapids, Minnesota, prohibiting photographers from entering the hospital. Likewise, copies of any pleadings or answers submitted by the press to the Judge's order should likewise be secured and forwarded to the bureau at an early date.

Very truly yours,
John Edgar Hoover – Director

September 4, 1938

Sunday

    Around 4:30 p.m., John Couch escapes from the Ramsey County Jail by removing several bricks under a window behind a locked door on one end of the cell block and squeezing through the hole and dropping about ten feet to the sidewalk.

Ramsey County Jail

    Jailers Herman Johnson and Hugh Schuck said they had seen him in his cellblock, apparently contented, less than half an hour before. They then went to dinner in an office nearby.

    Couch was confined in a block of four cells on the ground floor with four other prisoners. Jailers said the cell doors were not locked and opened out into a corridor, so that the prisoners could exercise when they chose.

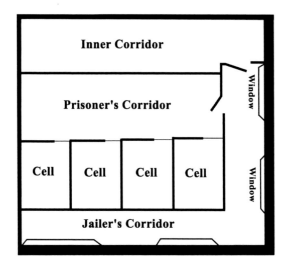

At one end of the corridor was a fine wire mesh,
holding the prisoners five feet from the steel-barred windows.
In the center of the mesh was a locked door.

Couch was able to open this door to work at removing
the bricks from under the steel barred windows.

Couch had been removing the mortar from around the
bricks for several days using only the metal spoon he was
issued when he entered the jail.

Harold Crieger, who was sunning himself in a second
floor window of the Palmer Hotel, right across from the jail at
44-1/2 West Fourth Street, saw the figure of a man outlined for
a moment against a window of the Ramsey County Jail. Then
he saw this same figure drop to the ground and dart off into
Kellogg Boulevard's busy traffic.

Mr. Crieger notified the Sheriff's office, and the hunt
was on.

Simulation of Couch's escape

Couch tries to commandeer a vehicle being driven by Henrietta Wallrich of St. Paul. As Couch jumps on the running board of her car, Miss Wallrich steps on the gas accelerating away. The doors are locked, and Couch can't force his way in, so he jumps off and heads toward the Mississippi river.

"I wasn't much frightened until I learned later that the man was a kidnaper," Miss Wallrich said.

Just before 5:00 p.m., St. Paul Police Chief Clinton Hackert phones Special Agent Berens to inform him about Couch's escape.

Two employees of the railroad roundhouse believe they saw Couch in the rail yards around 5:00 p.m.

Robert Hendon, Head of the St. Paul office of the FBI, is notified of the escape and orders all agents into the case.

Couch is now wanted on three charges, all federal offenses; transporting an automobile across a state line in violation of the Dyer Act, violation of the Lindbergh Kidnap Law, and violation of the Escaped Prisoner Act.

George Martin, of 471 Broadway, St. Paul, told police that he saw Couch at about 6:30 p.m. in the vicinity of the railroad yards. "The man appeared nervous," Martin said, "and asked about trains."

Martin reported the incident to police and identified a picture of Couch.

A detail led by Police Chief Clinton Hackert and Assistant Chief Charles Tierney searched the yards, but Couch could not be found.

"Couch is as dangerous as Dillinger ever was," said Chief Hackert. "His first act probably will be to get a gun. It is hard to tell what may happen then."

All freight trains leaving St. Paul are stopped at various points to search for Couch. Freight yards are checked.

Couch's description is announced on State Police radio station KNHD in Redwood Falls and commercial radio stations in the Twin Cities, WCCO, KSTP and WTCN.

Fearing that Couch might try to make his getaway by kidnapping some motorist, Chief Hackert warns drivers to have their car doors locked and not to pick up any hitchhikers.

Ramsey County Sheriff Thomas Gibbons, who was at Osakis, Minnesota, with his family, returns to St. Paul late Sunday night and immediately issues orders that all prisoners be confined inside cellblocks until the escape has been thoroughly investigated.

"The news of the escape," Gibbons told reporters, "was like getting hit between the eyes with a bat."

Motioning to a life-sized cutout of boxer Jack Dempsey, Gibbons said, "That guy couldn't hit."

Sheriff Gibbons had an earlier career as a professional boxer and had battled Jack Dempsey for the full fifteen rounds on July 4th, 1923 in Shelby, Montana. Dempsey won by decision.

**Jack Dempsey and Tommy Gibbons
Shelby, Montana 1923**

"I know it sounds like an alibi, but this isn't a jail. It's 47 years old, and in parts of it the masonry is badly in need of repair. I knew that when the kidnapers Barker, Karpis and those fellows were in here, but I was afraid to say it because I couldn't let them know it."

11:00 p.m.

The St. Paul Police Department is notified by Russell E. Amlee, of 716 Dayton Avenue, Apt. 5, St. Paul, that his 1933 Ford Coupe had been stolen that evening in Hudson, Wisconsin.

September 5, 1938

Monday

6:00 a.m.

Russell Amlee's stolen auto is discovered parked at the intersection of Western and Thomas in St. Paul by Police Patrolmen Alfred Wickoren and L. L. Byrne. Couch is found slouched down under the dash inside. He offers no resistance, and is not armed.

The officers bring him to the St. Paul Police Headquarters around 6:40 a.m.

During his ride to the Public Safety Building, Couch asks if he can comb his hair.

"If you make one move, you'll be a dead kidnapper," Wickoren tells him.

Couch has a comb in his pocket, but does not attempt to use it.

Couch is turned over to Sheriff Thomas Gibbons and placed in the Ramsey County Jail between around 7:30 a.m. He is then interviewed by Gibbons and Agent Hardy.

To reach the first floor jail window out of which he made his escape, it was necessary for him to get through a locked steel mesh door.

"I made a key that would fit it," Couch says. "After I got out, I threw the key away."

Surly and hardboiled, Couch refuses to tell more, out of what material he had made the key, how he had manufactured it, or any other details. He is difficult to question, gruffly declining to answer many queries and lapsing into periods of morose silence. When he does talk, however, he tells his story.

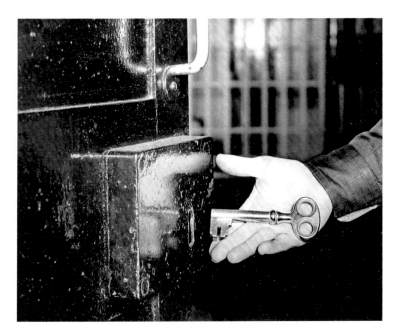

Lock and key to corridor door

On one occasion, a jailer had left a key in the door to the barred windows on the outside of the building.

Couch got a piece of soap and made an impression of the key. He then took the heavy metal handle from his drinking cup, straightened it out, and made a key by filing it with a nail file. He used a large metal spoon and a heavy iron catch about 6 inches long which holds the steel bunks to the cell wall, to dig the mortar out from around the bricks.

**Jailer Herman Johnston showing the
door to the escape window**

The spoon with which Couch affected his escape was a type customarily left in the prisoner's cells. It was made of soft metal and officials expressed surprise that he was able to use it effectively. This spoon was given to Couch when he first entered the jail on August 17th, it being the only utensil allowed him.

The spoon was found near the window, bearing marks to show it had been used for scraping was scarcely bent.

The last time the screened door leading to the window had been opened was at 7:00 p.m. Saturday.

Sheriff Gibbons at the point of the breakout

Couch states that in some instances he had to work for some time to remove a single brick. He says that none of the other prisoners were aware of his activities and that he made himself antagonistic to them, so that they would stay away from him.

Couch was able to remove enough bricks on September 4th to remove a marble slab, which allowed him access to the outside window. A Salvation Army band was playing in the block, which allowed him some cover. He pushed out the metal grating on the outside of the window, squeezed through and dropped about ten feet to the ground.

After jumping out of the jail window, Couch crossed Kellogg Boulevard and went down the hill past the Northern States Power Company plant.

"I found a manhole in the railroad yards down there and took off the cover. Then I climbed in and pulled the cover over the top. Then I crawled out and hooked a train out of town, riding on the cowcatcher, around 6:18 p.m., which took me to Hudson, Wisconsin."

At Hudson, Couch laid low in the weeds until darkness, and made his way to a frame house on the edge of town where he saw a 1933 Ford Coupe with the ignition keys in it. He drove the car around Hudson, and meant to head south back to Missouri, but got mixed up and headed west toward St. Paul. John entered a toll bridge over the St. Croix River. He drove right past the toll attendant, who tried to wave him down.

When he got to St. Paul, he tried to find his way out of town but ran out of gas, and he had no money. He was sleeping in the car when the officers found him.

Amlee said that he purchased the car June 13, 1938, from the Lewis Motor Company in St. Paul. The car was stolen from the back yard of his father-in-law O. C. Gullickson's house, in the 1200 block of 2nd street in Hudson about 9:30 p.m.

Amlee said that he saw his car being driven up St. Croix Avenue about 9:45 p.m. across Second Street in Hudson.

Amlee, thinking it was his brother-in-law using the car, yelled, "Hey Jim, where are you going with my car?" The driver, who had been driving slowly, stopped the car, then immediately drove away.

About 30 minutes later, Amlee learned that his brother-in-law was in St. Paul. He then reported his car as stolen.

•••

John R. Kahl escaped from the Ramsey County jail three days before Couch had. He also used a spoon to loosen bricks around a barred window, squirmed through the opening and dropped to the ground.

Couch's escape was simpler than Kahl's, who had been lodged on the fourth floor. Couch was housed on the first floor.

Kahl was arrested by federal agents on August 15th, in Kansas City, Missouri, and charged with the theft of a check in a letter. He was brought back to St. Paul for trial and was lodged by himself on the fourth floor of the jail. Thursday, September 1st, about 7:30 p.m. he escaped using a tablespoon to dig under the masonry between the window and window bars and letting himself down with a series of sheets tied together into a rope.

At the time of Couch's escape, the four other prisoners in his cell block were paying little attention to him, insisting that they didn't know of his escape until he was gone. One of prisoners was ill, and the others were talking to him as he lay on his cell bunk.

"Couch would never speak to us," one of the prisoners said. "When we were let into the corridors, he went off by himself. We tried to cheer him up a couple of times and brought him candy, but he still wouldn't have anything to do with us."

•••

It was in the Ramsey County Jail that three other federal prisoners had committed suicide in recent years.

Willie Sharkey, one of the four Touhy Gang members acquitted in the William Hamm Kidnapping (President of Hamm's Brewing Co.), was found dead in his cell December 1, 1933. With two neckties given to him by his brother, he fashioned a noose with which he hanged himself. The suicide took place as Sharkey and his companions, though freed of the Hamm charges, awaited removal to Chicago to face charges of kidnapping John (Jake the Barber) Factor.

Jack Peifer, night club operator of St. Paul, took poison after receiving up to 30 years for his part in the Hamm kidnapping, a crime for which members of the Karpis-Barker gang were convicted. He was found dead awaiting transportation from St. Paul to the Federal Penitentiary at Leavenworth, Kansas, on July 31, 1936.

The third death was that of Ralph Gibson, confessed bank robber and suspected murderer. Gibson was being taken to a second floor cell after conferring with his attorney on August 14, 1937. He broke away from a jailer and bolted for a nearby stairway. He ran up towards the fourth floor, found a locked gate barring his way and then leaped over a banister landing three flights below. He was under a sentence of up to forty years for bank robberies in Eyota and Cold Spring, Minnesota.

•••

Chief Jailer Emery Clewett of the Ramsey County Jail, along with Assistant Jailers Hugh Schuck and Herman Johnston are interviewed by the FBI.

Couch had been in Tank #1, about 10 feet above street level. His cell door was not locked, and he was allowed freedom in the corridor with the other prisoners in front of his cell.

There were four other prisoners in the cellblock with Couch when he escaped; Joe Levine, Robert Coleman, George Albert Hessler and Thomas Quinn.

Levine was allowed to mop the corridor outside the cellblock early in the morning on September 4th. The mesh door leading to the window was open at this time because this is the area where they stored the cleaning supplies. Around 8:30 a.m., Jailer Johnson asks Levine if he was done, and Levine told him that he was. Couch said to him, "What are you telling them to close that door for? Are you a Copper too?"

Coleman and Hessler said that they did not know Couch was planning an escape and knew very little about him.

Quinn said that on September 2nd, 3rd and 4th, all that Couch would talk about was killing somebody, and that he seemed to be looking for trouble with the other prisoners. Couch would pace the floor and try to pick arguments with them. For this reason, the others stayed away from him.

Jailer Clewett says the only person that Couch had been friendly with in jail was Leon Gleckman, a prisoner who was released on August 24th.

Gleckman was contacted by the FBI, and he told them that Couch had no money, was desperate, and that he would not let anyone stand in the way of his escape. Couch would kill before he would be taken alive. Couch told him that he even intends on killing his own brother, Russell, who had been a witness against another brother, George, for murdering a policeman in St. Louis, Missouri.

•••

Because Couch took advantage of the music of a religious group to cover the noise of his escape, such services will be banned in the future. "The singing is very nice, but you can't hear anything else while it is going on," Sheriff Gibbons said.

•••

On being returned to the Ramsey County Jail, Couch is placed in the same cell he had occupied before, but precautions are taken to preclude another break. A handcuff is clamped on one wrist and attached by a steel chain to the wall. Sheriff Gibbons states that the prisoner will remain chained in this manner until his removal.

The Sheriff also said Couch will remain locked in his cell during his entire stay in the jail, not being allowed the liberty of the corridor in front of the cell tier. Also, none of the other prisoners in the block will be permitted to use the prisoner's corridor.

Sheriff Gibbons in Couch's Cell

With these precautions in place, Gibbons points out that Couch will have to free himself from his handcuff and break through steel doors if he wishes to escape again.

September 6, 1938

Tuesday

J. Edgar Hoover sends a telegraph of congratulations to the St. Paul Police Department for the capture of John Couch.

I DESIRE TO EXPRESS TO YOU MY COMMENDATION FOR THE SPLENDID WORK OF PATROLMEN ALFRED WICKOREN AND L. L. BYRNE IN EFFECTING THE APPREHENSION OF JOHN COUCH, THE PROMPT APPREHENSION OF THIS ESCAPED PRISONER IS AN EXCEPTIONAL EXAMPLE OF THE MERIT OF COOPERATION IN LAW ENFORCEMENT AND A SPLENDID EXAMPLE OF POLICE EFFICIENCY.

September 7, 1938

Wednesday

A list of recommendations for repairs to prevent a recurrence of the "tablespoon escape" from the Ramsey County Jail is drawn up by Sheriff Thomas J. Gibbons.

The Sheriff also plans to frustrate escapes by withholding meal utensils from dangerous prisoners, serving them instead with paper plates and cardboard cutlery.

The recommendations will be submitted Thursday at a special meeting of the County Commissioners, with the request that the board make the improvements at once.

The proposals are:

-installation of steel window frames and steel plate reinforcing around the windowsills.

-New concrete filling around the windows.

-Resetting in cement of the wall tiles, now in lime.

-Replacement or removal of loose stone in the cornices.

These repairs were recommended after the building had been inspected by Harry Bronson, County Surveyor; Ade Dreher, General Construction Superintendent for the Department of Parks, Playgrounds and Public Buildings; and Sheriff Gibbons.

September 10, 1938

Saturday

John R. Kahl, 18, who escaped from the Ramsey County Jail on September 1st, is captured in Kansas City, Missouri.

He was originally brought to St. Paul from Kansas City, Missouri, to face federal mail theft charges. Postal workers say he stole a check from a St. Paul mailbox.

September 12, 1938

Monday

An order is issued to appoint counsel for John Couch.

September 19, 1938

Monday

Assistant FBI Director Harold Nathan writes to SAC Hendon in St. Paul regarding the newspaper photographer taking the photo of Meredith being fingerprinted. He again requests that they forward a copy of the restraining order secured by the County Attorney at Grand Rapids, Minnesota, prohibiting photographers from entering the hospital, along with any pleadings or answers submitted by the press to the judge's order.

September 20, 1938

Tuesday

St. Paul, Minnesota

The US Government begins presentation to a Grand Jury evidence against John Couch, seeking indictments under the Lindbergh Law and Federal Escaped Prisoners Act.

US District Attorney Victor E. Anderson presents the case, the first to be heard by this Grand Jury.

Daniel Cox Fahey, Jr. testifies for an hour in the morning, followed by six FBI agents who give additional testimony.

Miss Gross was not subpoenaed for the Grand Jury.

Sheriff Gibbons testifies regarding Couch's jailbreak.

In the Grand Jury system neither the defendant nor his counsel are present during witnesses' testimony.

The jury may stipulate the death sentence under the Lindbergh Kidnap Act, but DA Anderson does not demand it.

Another case before the grand jury today is that charging a St. Paul contracting company with breach of WPA regulations for carrying out a contract.

The Secret Service Agents present to give testimony regarding alleged forgeries of WPA checks came to St. Paul directly from Rochester, Minnesota, where they had the duty of guarding President Roosevelt and members of his family while they were visiting the President's son, James, who is recuperating from a surgery to remove a stomach ulcer.

September 21, 1938

Wednesday

The US Federal Court designates Kleve J. Flakne to represent John Couch.

Flakne was Mayor of the Twin Cities' suburb St. Louis Park from 1932 to 1933.

Kleve J. Flakne

September 22, 1938

Thursday

Couch is indicted by the Federal Grand Jury, under the Lindbergh Law, for kidnapping Viola Cecelia (Peggy) Gross and Daniel Cox Fahey, Jr. of St. Louis, Missouri on August 13th.

The Grand Jury also indicted Couch under the Federal Escape Act for breaking out of the Ramsey County Jail September 4th.

US Attorney Victor Anderson says he will likely ask for a life sentence, instead of the death penalty, for John Couch when the alleged kidnapper answers the charges in Federal Court in Minneapolis September 27th.

In this connection, the indictment omitted any references to the injury Fahey allegedly suffered when accosted by Couch and Meredith. Fahey is alleged to have been struck in the nose with the butt of a gun.

John Kahl, earlier Ramsey County Jail escapee, is also indicted today by the Grand Jury for theft from the mails, as well as for escaping from jail.

Also during this Grand Jury, the Federal Campaign Against Indecent Literature obtained an indictment containing five counts against Antoinette Fawcett, Phil Rolfson and the Bob Edwards Publishing Company. The bills involve the magazines Calgary Eye-Opener, Old Nick's Annual T.N.T. and Eye-Opener's Annual Red Pepper, all of which contained allegedly lewd pictures.

•••

SAC Hendon advises Washington that Couch was indicted today for the Gross/Fahey kidnapping by a St. Paul Grand Jury, and was also indicted for the St. Paul jailbreak under the Federal Escape Act. Bond is set at $100,000.

September 23, 1938

Friday

John Couch is examined by a Psychiatrist.

September 27, 1938

Tuesday

John Couch pleads innocent in Federal Court to kidnapping Daniel Cox Fahey, Jr., and Viola Gross. Kleve Flakne, Couch's court appointed counsel, reserved the right to change the plea and hints a possible insanity defense, saying he does not know what his plan of action will be until he has seen the psychiatric report.

Flakne states that several years ago, while serving in a Missouri Prison, Couch was struck in the head by a guard and still bears a scar.

Trial is set for Monday, October 3rd.

Couch is committed to custody of the Sheriff of Hennepin County.

•••

Floyd Hamilton was sentenced to serve 20 years in the Texas State Penitentiary for robbery with firearms.

When a District Court jury returned its verdict against Hamilton last night, he turned to Judge George Adams and said, "Judge, that may be more than I can do."

Hamilton was the second member of his family to become the No. 1 man on the FBI's Most Wanted list. He was convicted in the same courtroom in which the death sentence was accorded to his brother Raymond in 1935.

Authorities announced that Hamilton would be held in jail in Dallas before federal officials would transfer him to Texarkana, Arkansas, to stand trial on charges of robbery of the Bradley, Arkansas bank.

Hamilton was indicted in the Federal Judicial District of Texarkana on the bank case. His case is docketed there for the November term of the Court.

District Attorney Andrew Patten announced that he was ready today to try Huron Ted Walters, Hamilton's companion, on a similar robbery charge.

Walters will then be transferred to Texarkana with Hamilton for trial in federal court, where he is also indicted.

September 28, 1938

Wednesday

US Attorney Victor Anderson announces officially that the death penalty will not be asked for John Couch.

Anderson said that the Attorney General's office in Washington has instructed him not to seek such a penalty.

Couch pleaded not guilty in federal court in Minneapolis Tuesday. Unless he changes his plea, he will go to trial Monday.

October 3, 1938

Monday

UNITED STATES v JOHN COUCH

FEDERAL COURT CASE 6812

Minneapolis, Minnesota

Judge: Matthew M. Joyce
US District Attorney: Victor E. Anderson
Couch's Attorney: Kleve J. Flakne

The government had previously announced that it would not press for the death sentence. As a consequence, Couch faces a sentence of up to life if convicted.

US District Attorney Victor E. Anderson states to the court the criminal record of the defendant, citing the times and places he had escaped from custody (at least four times). He moves the court that the defendant be handcuffed to a Deputy Marshal during the process of this trial, which said motion is granted by the court.

Couch shouts out, "No, no," to a statement made by Anderson that Couch was a desperado and associated with dangerous characters. Prospective jurors have not yet been brought into the courtroom for examination when this interruption occurs.

Kleve J. Flakne, Couch's Court appointed counsel, now moves that the statement made by Mr. Anderson be stricken from the record. Exception allowed.

Deputy Marshal Sinclair and John Couch

Mr. Flakne moves that the jury, after being empanelled and sworn, be held in custody during the trial, and with Mr. Anderson joining in counsel's request, it is so ordered.

Jury selection begins.

JURORS:
Harry W. Swanson - Watertown
Martin E. Dunn - Anoka
Joseph J. Stumvoll - Becker
Martin Friis - Porter
Sam Hess - Howard Lake
Erling Johnson - Luverne
N.A. Johnson - Cedar
Louis H. Prickett - Buffalo
Olaf Hegstad - Slayton
Roy E. Butman - Pipestone
Mrs. C. J. Lindenberg - Chaska
Herbert E. Swanson - Bethel

Prospective jurors excused by the Court were D. D. Stringer of Canby and Ed Lindberg of Hector.

The US excused prospective jurors Leo F. Fischer of Lafayette, Mrs. J. W. Lindblom of Worthington, Mrs. Frank Neuman, Sr. of St. James, and Florence Foster of Waseca.

The Defense excused only Raymond D. Healy of Minneapolis.

The jurors are sworn.

Jurors list filed.

Officers are sworn to keep the jury in custody.

Mr. Anderson opens and states case.

Mr. Flakne moves for mistrial on the account of a prejudicial statement made by Mr. Anderson in his opening statement. Motion denied.

Daniel Cox Fahey, Jr. is sworn for the plaintiff.

Fahey identifies John Couch as his kidnapper, and then tells the court of the 24 hour flight in which he and Miss Peggy Gross were taken by Couch.

John Couch sits calmly as Fahey identifies him as one of the kidnappers, in contrast to his earlier outbursts.

Fahey testifies that Couch slammed the car door on his foot.

Fahey testifies that he believes that Couch was the man who struck him with the butt of a gun when the kidnappers jumped on the running board of his car and forced him and Miss Gross into the back seat.

He also testifies that both Couch and Meredith fired at him when he and Miss Gross failed to return to the car quickly enough after stopping for food.

Fahey describes the trip from St. Louis to Minnesota in detail. He says the kidnappers bragged of their various criminal exploits, and often took shots at telephone poles to emphasize parts of their story.

He states that they stopped several times for food and water.

On cross-examination, Kleve Flakne points out that it was Meredith, and not Couch, who drove the Fahey car when it was crossing state borders. Fahey said that Couch drove but a half hour, several hours after the abduction.

Fahey testifies that with the exception of the time he was struck on the nose, and his ankle was slammed in the car door, and when Couch swung his fist at him, that the men did not mistreat them, and that they stopped several times along the way for food and drink. Fahey says that he joked with Couch and Meredith on the trip.

Court is adjourned until Tuesday morning.

October 4, 1938

Tuesday

Daniel Cox Fahey, Jr. is recalled for the plaintiff.

Fahey testifies that Couch acknowledged him in court on Monday. "Yes I saw him. He spoke to me in the hallway."

Anderson asks Fahey what Couch had said to him.

Fahey states that he said, "Hi Dan. Give me a break, will you?" This provokes a chuckle in the courtroom.

Fahey testifies that on the way to Minneapolis, Couch mentioned that he used to be a boxer in Iowa. Fahey suggested that they stop the car and, "make a sporting proposition of it." Fahey offered that if Couch and Meredith would throw down their guns, he would go into the woods with them and they would settle it with fists, two against one.

The kidnappers declined the offer.

Victor Anderson questions Fahey as to whether there had been any talk about Dillinger on the ride from St. Louis.

Over the objection of Kleve Flakne, Fahey is permitted to answer.

"Couch said Dillinger had traveled this road many times," Fahey stated. "They remarked they would be tougher than Dillinger."

Couch raises up his hand that is manacled to the Marshal and shouts, "This is evidence of prejudice."

Kleve Flakne asks that the conversation relating to Dillinger on the trip up to Minneapolis be left out of the evidence because it is prejudicial.

The attorneys argue over the asserted statement by Couch that, "Dillinger used this road."

While Flakne and Anderson are arguing about the Dillinger conversation at the bench, Couch calls out, "That has nothing to do with bringing him (Fahey) up here."

Fahey testifies that he had been struck across the face, and was also shot at by Couch when he was slow in obeying a command.

Fahey said that when he was left in the woods near Champlin, that Couch came over and shook hands with him and wished him luck. "I wished him luck too," Fahey says.

Flakne's cross-examination of Fahey indicates that he is attempting to prove that Couch was only a dupe for Meredith.

Viola C. Gross is sworn for the plaintiff.

"Peggy" Gross identifies John Couch as one of her kidnappers.

Miss Gross testifies that shortly after they were kidnapped, Couch turned around to them in the car and asked her if she had ever heard of Couch and Meredith. She replied that she had not, and Couch told her a long story of his and Meredith's exploits.

John Couch listens with eyes downcast as Miss Gross tells her story of the abduction, which is similar to the one Fahey had previously related.

When asked by Flakne as to whether the defendant had treated her as a gentleman should, Miss Gross replies, "No, not the entire trip."

Miss Gross states that while being bound by Couch near Champlin, Minnesota, that he had, "made a proposal."

Couch shakes his head vigorously.

"When Couch made a proposal, I became frightened and I screamed for Meredith. Meredith came over and said he would shoot Couch if he touched me," Miss Gross testifies.

She says that as Couch and Meredith left them after tying them up, that they wished her good luck. "We wished them good luck, too."

Carl Gustafson is sworn for the plaintiff.

Gustafson, a farmer who lives near Champlin, states that he and Roland Reilly drove about 200 feet past the point where they first heard the cries for help before turning back.

Gustafson, who picked up Fahey and Gross after they were left in the woods, describes releasing the wire that was binding the couple and taking them to his home and calling the Sheriff's Office in Minneapolis.

Roland C. Reilly is sworn for the plaintiff.

Reilly reiterates Gustafson's story of finding Fahey and Gross.

FBI Special Agent Samuel W. Hardy is sworn for the plaintiff.

A statement which Hardy took from Couch on August 16, 1938, in which he admitted the abduction of Daniel Fahey and Miss Peggy Gross, is read to the jury.

Couch fidgets while the statement is read, but on advice from his counsel, he refrains from the outbursts which had marked the trial Monday afternoon and Tuesday morning.

The five-page statement was written by Hardy and signed by Couch in the presence of other officers.

Hardy testifies that Couch readily admitted the kidnapping, but told him, "You aren't going to clear up a whole lot of cases on me."

FBI Special Agent Roy T. Noonan is sworn for the plaintiff and gives testimony.

During a break in the trial, a little old woman asks Clerk of Court Chell Smith to direct her to Couch's attorney. He leads her over to Kleve Flakne.

"I'm from the south," she explains, rather timidly. "I think I know some of the things this boy has been up against. I'd like to help him."

She gives Flakne a dollar bill. "Give this to him," she says. "Let him get a haircut and buy himself some cigarettes."

The government is expected to complete its case Wednesday morning.

Court is adjourned to Wednesday, October 5th, at 10:00 a.m.

October 5, 1938

Wednesday

John Couch appears in court in a new tie and shirt, and wearing socks for the first time. He is sporting a fresh haircut too, paid for by the sympathetic woman who had given a dollar to his attorney the day before.

Special Agent Roy T. Noonan is recalled for the plaintiff.

Frank A. Archambo, one of the Hennepin County Sheriff's Deputies who responded to the call from Carl Gustafson after he found Gross and Fahey bound along side the road, is sworn for the plaintiff.

Stanley Hurley, a Hennepin County Sheriff's Deputy who was present when Fahey was interviewed at the FBI Office, is sworn for the plaintiff.

Edward R. Notesteen, FBI Special Agent, is sworn for the plaintiff.

Harry N. Lamson, Itasca County Deputy Sheriff of Effie, Minnesota, is sworn for the plaintiff.

Lamson quotes Couch as saying that he regretted not trying to shoot it out with federal agents when he was captured last August on a farm near Effie, Minnesota.

Lamson testifies that Couch had told him, "I'm sorry I didn't stick my hand in the window of the car. It would have been all over now. You'd have been a damn fool if you hadn't shot me. As it is, I've got the electric chair staring me in the face." Couch was referring to the handguns stored in the glove box of Fahey's car at the scene where they were abducted.

Lamson testifies that he asked Couch why he had not changed the license plates on the Fahey car. "He told me that he hadn't been out enough to know the ways of the world. He said he had been serving time in a reformatory and 'The Big House.' He told me, too, that the reason they went to the Rootes' farm was that Minneapolis was too hot for them. They were going to meet some party there."

Bigfork, Minnesota, Police Chief Glen P. Miller is sworn and testifies for the plaintiff.

James Otis Meredith's brother-in-law, Roy L. Rootes, of Effie, Minnesota, is sworn for the plaintiff.

Rootes testifies that Meredith and Couch came to the farm of his father, Charles Rootes, near Effie, Minnesota, early Sunday morning, August 14th.

He then testifies of the shooting of Meredith and the capture of Couch on August 15th.

Rootes states that, when captured, Couch readily admitted the kidnapping when accused of it by Agent S. W. Hardy.

Mrs. Gladys Rootes, Meredith's Mother-in-law, is sworn and testifies for the plaintiff.

The plaintiff rests his case.

Immediately after the government rested it's case, Kleve Flakne opens and states the case for the defendant.

Flakne tells the jury that Couch was under the influence of liquor when he and Meredith accosted the St. Louis couple in a parked car in Clayton, a suburb of St. Louis.

John Couch is sworn on his own behalf.

Couch, quietly and without much movement of his lips, tells how he had spent most of his time in reformatories and the Missouri State Prison since he left school in the sixth grade. He testifies that he has not been out of a penal institution for more than three months at a time. He admits he ran away from reformatories three times (probably more), and that he suffered a skull fracture when he was hit on the head for refusal to work at the Missouri State Prison. His sentences were for car thefts and burglaries.

Couch states that on August 12th, he and Meredith drank whiskey and were hitchhiking out of St. Louis, planning to go north for jobs in the harvest fields. Early in the morning of August 13th, Meredith spotted the Fahey car.

Couch says that he and Meredith had attended a band concert on the evening of August 12th.

Couch states that he acted on the instructions of Meredith in jumping on the running board of the Fahey car and ordering the couple to the rear compartment. When asked where he received the gun he carried, Couch says that Meredith gave him the .32 caliber revolver.

"We were going to hitchhike, and he said we should have guns for our own protection," Couch states. "We planned to do a little hunting."

Couch admits to abducting Daniel Fahey and Peggy Gross from St. Louis and transporting them to Minneapolis. He adds that he didn't think it was kidnapping, as charged, but merely the stealing of a car.

"If it were kidnapping we wouldn't have left them in a field, if we wanted to get ransom."

Couch denies shooting at Fahey, and he also denies making improper advances toward Miss Gross.

The session ends with another brief outburst by Couch. On cross-examination by Victor Anderson, he is asked if he had kidnapped a man named Kalousek at Greenwood, Missouri.

"If you are getting that from a statement the officers got from me in the Ramsey Jail, well, they pestered me and antagonized me," Couch relates vigorously, "I told them anything to get them away."

"You intentionally gave false information to the officers?"
Victor Anderson asks.

"Yes," Couch answers.

"Your Honor," Couch says, raising his voice and turning to
Judge Joyce, "what am I being tried for?"

"Hasn't your attorney told you?" Judge Joyce questions, which
draws a chuckle from the courtroom.

"Yes," Couch replies.

The questioning of Couch on another kidnapping arose as a
result of his denial on direct examination that he had ever
participated in any other kidnapping or had bound any other
victims.

Judge Joyce then adjourns the trial to 10:00 a.m. Thursday.

The case is likely to go to the Jury of eleven men and a woman
on Thursday.

OCTOBER 6, 1938

Thursday

John Couch is recalled on his own behalf.

Couch denies a statement made in one of his interviews by the
FBI, which mentioned abduction of a man named Kalousek at
Greenwood, Missouri, and leaving him tied up near the
Boonville Reformatory. He also denies that he and Otis
Meredith took a car from a man named Davenport in Texas, or
that they picked up two girl hitchhikers and drove them to

"Did you sign this statement?" Anderson demands, showing a statement taken by Special Agent Samuel W. Hardy in the Ramsey County Jail.

"That's my signature," Couch snaps, "but I didn't say those things that are in there. If I signed it, I didn't know they were in there."

Sentence by sentence, the prosecutor reads the statement in the presence of the jury with Couch denying every word.

"Did you say that?" Anderson demands.

"No," Couch snaps back each time.

Couch admits forcing Daniel Cox Fahey, Jr. and Miss Peggy Gross to accompany him and Otis Meredith in Fahey's car from St. Louis to Champlin, Minnesota. There, he testifies, he helped truss them up with wire and left them in a field. Again he insists that he doesn't think it was kidnapping but merely stealing a car.

Carl Gustafson is recalled for the Defense.

The defense rests.

FBI Special Agent Samuel W. Hardy is recalled for the plaintiff in rebuttal.

Emory J. Clewett, Chief Jailer of the Ramsey County Jail, is sworn for the plaintiff in rebuttal.

The plaintiff rests and testimony is closed.

Victor Anderson states that the evidence is most clear that Couch effected kidnapping as defined in the Lindbergh Law and termed unreasonable a plea to free him.

Testimony shows that Couch and Meredith came north from St. Louis to do a job in north Minneapolis but found it too hot.

They then went to the farm of Meredith's father-in-law near Effie, Minnesota, where Couch was caught and Meredith was shot.

US District Attorney Anderson closes.

Kleve Flakne, in a final plea to the jury, says that Couch did not knowingly effect the kidnapping. Flakne cites testimony in which Couch said that he was drinking on the night of August 12th, a few hours before Miss Gross and Fahey were abducted in Fahey's car. Flakne also reiterates Couch's testimony that he had a headache a few hours before accosting the victims and took a pill given to him by Meredith.

"Couch was merely a dupe for Meredith," Flakne states. "He fell asleep a short time after the trip started, and when he awoke, he didn't know where he was. He drove the car only a short time and didn't know he was committing the crime of kidnapping."

Flakne points out that Couch has freely testified to transporting the St. Louis couple to a field near Champlin, Minnesota, and binding them with wire. He states that it is a clear violation of the Dyer Act which applies to transportation of stolen cars interstate.

Flakne points out that Couch, 23, has spent nearly all of the past nine years in Missouri reformatories and is on probation in Missouri. He already faces a continuation of his sentence of 1932.

Mr. Flakne closes.

Judge Joyce, in charging the jury with the case, states that its only duty is to determine the guilt or innocence of John Couch.

The case is sent to the jury at 5:10 p.m. Thirty-five minutes later they go out to dinner. They return to deliberations at 7:50 p.m. and they reach a verdict at 9:20 p.m. Then they are locked up for the night in the Andrews Hotel.

Judge Joyce had said he would hear a verdict if it were reached by 9:00 p.m., but the decision came 20 minutes late.

The verdict will not be revealed until Friday morning.

October 7, 1938

Friday

John Couch is brought back to the Courtroom around 10:00 a.m. His right hand is manacled to Deputy United States Marshal Earl Sinclair.

Couch carefully watches the door through which Judge M. M. Joyce will enter until he comes through it and appears at the bench.

Clerk of Court Chell Smith reads the verdict.

United States District Court, District of Minnesota

........F̶O̶U̶R̶T̶H̶........ DIVISION

THE UNITED STATES OF AMERICA,

Plaintiff,

against

JOHN COUCH

Defendant

Verdict

We, the Jury in the above-entitled action,

do find the defendant, JOHN COUCH .... GUILTY AS CHARGED IN THE INDICTMENT.

DATED:- OCTOBER 6, 1938

, Foreman.

N.A. Johnson

"We, the Jury in the above-entitled action, do find the defendant, John Couch, guilty as charged in the indictment. N.A. Johnson, Foreman."

Couch's gaze switches from Smith to the jury, as Foreman N. A. Johnson acknowledges the verdict.

Couch raises his left hand and thumbs his nose and waggles his fingers at the jury, shouting, "Thank you."

Judge Joyce thanks the jury for its services. "I think this is a just verdict. I don't see how it could have been otherwise. You have met your civic responsibility and the community is indebted to you."

Just as Judge Joyce is about to announce sentence, US Attorney Victor Anderson rises with a motion that the sentencing be stayed until an investigation can be made by the Probation Department. He states that information has come to his office since the close of the trial which the court should know about.

Couch's counsel Kleve Flakne is on his feet at the same time, and states that he was about to make the same motion, the basis of which neither Attorney discloses.

The Court refers the case to probation officers pending sentencing, which is set for 9:30 a.m. Monday.

October 9, 1938

Sunday

John Couch is interviewed in the Hennepin County Jail by Chief US Probation Officer Ernest J. Meili from 9:30 a.m. until 12:15 p.m.

In his summary, Meili notes that Couch was born in St. Louis, Missouri, 23 years ago. He grew up in poverty as a result of his Father's addiction to alcohol. His mother died when he was 15 years old. He has a 6th grade education, good health, and no financial assets. He associates with prostitutes, drinks excessively and gambles.

Meili notes that Couch has been in and out of the courts since age 10. He adds that it may be the fact that time after time he was given probation may have encouraged him in wrongdoing, rather than acting as a deterrent. Since 1931, he had been continuously incarcerated with the exception of a period from June 9, 1938, until his arrest August 15, 1938, in this case.

Meili discusses in his report his own post-graduate work at the State Prison of Missouri in 1920. He calls it a breeding place for crime. It is characterized by filth, unspeakable brutality, and exploitation of the worst kind.

Meili states that there is no question that the treatment received at the prison made Couch worse and gave him a decidedly warped attitude toward life and society.

Couch denies that he engaged in any crime except this kidnapping and car theft, and denies any statements made in the document he signed on August 24th.

Meili notes that Couch was very cooperative during the interview, and did not reveal any vicious tendencies. He adds that, *"It is debatable to what extent Couch was a victim of poor environment, poor heredity and prison brutality, but that this is mostly an academic question. There cannot be any doubt that we are dealing with a very dangerous individual whose mind is warped and who in all probability will always be a menace to law abiding citizens. He expressed the wish that he had met the same fate as befell Meredieth. This might have been a merciful solution to this case."*

October 10, 1938

Monday

9:30 a.m.

Court resumes for Jon Couch's sentencing.

His verdict is read again.

John Couch is sentenced – Period of his natural life, penitentiary to be designated, for, "Transporting kidnapped persons in interstate commerce."

Minimum expected date: Life. Maximum expected date: Life. Parole date: October 9, 1953.

"You took a long chance, Couch, and lost," says Judge Joyce. "You are not smart, but you are cunning. You have been a menace to society. I believe you when you say that you did not kidnap for ransom, but you are guilty under the law, and I believe you would not have hesitated to shoot your way to freedom if you had the opportunity. Your crime is a new type of menace to society, and it must be scotched. Society is entitled to be protected from your kind."

"I am sincerely sorry for you," Judge Joyce goes on. "You've spent the last seven or eight years of your life in prison. You never had a normal boyhood. Whether there is much good left in you, it is pretty hard to say."

Couch receives the sentence with little show of emotion, though while he is being led out of the courtroom he murmurs that he, "didn't get a right shake, but I guess I'll have to make the best of it."

The United States Marshal's Office prepares to take Couch to Leavenworth Penitentiary for the usual quarantine period.

Couch will be eligible for parole in 15 years if his prison record proves good.

John Couch is delivered to the Hennepin County Jail to await transfer to Leavenworth, Kansas. He is not housed with the other federal prisoners, but is kept on the first tier with the state prisoners. Three extra guards are hired to watch Couch, each working eight-hour shifts.

October 11, 1938

St. Paul Special Agent In Charge Hendon replies to Washington's three requests for the restraining order barring reporters from entering the hospital where Meredith had been treated for his gunshot wounds. Washington had requested copies of the order on September 3rd, September 19th, and on October 5th.

A letter was forwarded to Itasca County Attorney John J. Benton on September 19th and on September 23rd regarding this matter, but no response was received. On September 27th, SAC Hendon attempted to personally contact Mr. Benton without success. On October 8th, SA Noonan interviewed Benton, who advised him that no restraining order had been issued on August 17, 1938, although at that time it had been discussed, and that he intended to get a restraining order out, but he could not determine to whom to direct it. In lieu thereof, he stated that he had a deputy placed on duty the following day at the hospital in Grand Rapids.

Benton said that he had called the St. Paul Dispatch and requested that they not print the photograph of Meredith which had been taken, but they reported that the paper had already gone to press.

Benton advised the St. Paul Dispatch that if their photographers appeared in Grand Rapids again, he would have them put in jail.

Hendon notes that prior to locating Benton, he had talked to Miss Mabel Korsell, Superintendent of the Itasca County Hospital at Grand Rapids, and Dr. J. L. McLeod, and they were both of the opinion that the county attorney had secured a restraining order. He had advised them that he had fixed the matter so that they would not be bothered further, and requested them to immediately call the sheriff if any photographers appeared at the hospital.

October 12, 1938

John Couch is delivered to the US Penitentiary in Leavenworth, Kansas.

November 3, 1938

Hamilton and Walters plead guilty in US District Court in Fort Smith, Arkansas, to the robbery of the Bank in Bradley, Arkansas, and of the Dyer Act, transporting a stolen vehicle across state lines.

They receive a 30-year sentence from Judge Heartsill Ragon.

Before sentencing, Hamilton approached the bench, saying, "Your Honor, I have a few words to say. I know I've been wrote up in the newspapers as being pretty bad, but, my actual criminal record, I haven't committed no crimes til last June. If you can show me any leniency, I'd appreciate it."

"My sympathies go to young men, but I can't find a single mitigating circumstance in your case," the Judge says.

"The trouble with too long a sentence," Hamilton replies, "is that when you get out you don't have no family, no friends. I'd like to get out and start again, straight."

Judge Ragon replies, "Have you ever thought that in your case it would be better if you didn't have any friends. You evidently have always had the wrong kind."

November 10, 1938

The Federal Grand Jury in Fort Worth, Texas, returns a No True Bill against Hattie May Bass and Ruth Baker. They will not have to stand trial.

November 16, 1938

James Clyde Reed is found guilty in Kennett, Missouri, of the armed holdup at the Bullock Farm near Holcomb, Missouri. He is sentenced to fifteen years in the Missouri State Penitentiary.

November 27, 1938

Daniel Cox Fahey, Jr. marries Virginia McBlair Garesche of St. Louis.

November 29, 1938

John Couch is transferred from Leavenworth to USP Alcatraz, in the San Francisco Bay of California.

Reason for transfer: *"Subject's criminal history indicates that he is a habitual criminal of a hardened and dangerous nature. He has a long sentence, has escaped from institutions three times and also has detainers filed against him. He made poor adjustments while serving sentences in other institutions and transfer is recommended with maximum supervision."*

Couch has no disciplinary reports from Leavenworth. He is assigned Alcatraz prisoner number 468.

In his intake evaluation, they record his IQ at 84, and his Stanford-Binet mental age rating at about 13 years, 6 months, which is about the same physical age at which he was first incarcerated. He is very concerned about the long sentence that he has received for what he considers an unimportant crime. He is not considered psychotic, but is emotionally inadequate.

December 2, 1938

The FBI concludes their investigation of an alleged attempted bank robbery in Texas claimed by Meredith on his deathbed.

No information could be obtained as to a possible attempted robbery in Clearwater, Texas (the place named by Meredith), Clear Lake, Texas, or anyplace else in Texas.

January 27, 1939

The FBI Office in San Francisco makes an attempt to interview John Couch in Alcatraz to try and clear up some pending cases in the Midwest.

Associate Warden E. J. Miller states that Couch is not available for interview, as he is now a patient in the prison hospital where he is under observation to ascertain whether or not he is insane. He is unable to furnish any information as to when Couch would be available for interview as he had been acting "queer" for some time.

Dr. Romney Ritchie, Chief Surgeon of Alcatraz Prison, is interviewed and states that he does not believe that it would be wise to interview Couch at this time, as he is now under observation and he is liable to "blow his top," if he were interviewed.

February 12, 1939

John Couch engages in a fistfight in the Alcatraz recreation yard with Harry Murry, inmate #464. Words were passed between them and then the fight broke out. They are sent to solitary confinement, with a restricted diet and no privileges until further notice.

February 16, 1939

John Couch is released from solitary confinement to idle in his cell with his privileges still withheld until further notice.

February 26, 1939

All privileges are restored to John Couch.

March 9, 1939

Alcatraz allows the San Francisco FBI Office to interview Couch to try clear up some open cases in the Midwest.

Couch denies any knowledge or participation in the holdups of the MotoGas Station in Barnhart, Missouri, on July 27, 1938; of the Big Chief Cabin Hotel in Pond, Missouri, on July 29, 1938; or of the St. Francois Recreation Club near Farmington, Missouri, on August 3, 1938.

Couch states that after being released from the Missouri State Penitentiary in Jefferson City, Missouri, on June 18, 1938, he met Meredith in St. Louis and they decided to go to Effie, Minnesota, to visit Meredith's wife.

They intended to try find employment at the CCC Camp where Meredith once worked. They took Fahey and Miss Gross in Fahey's car to Minnesota, where they left the two tied up outside of Champlin, just north of the Twin Cities.

Couch denies any knowledge of any other robberies, and states that he does not believe anyone could identify him as having taken part in any of the mentioned robberies.

Couch states he is aware that there is a detainer filed against him on a charge of armed robbery by Troop A, Missouri State Highway Patrol, Lee's Summit, Missouri.

Couch is difficult to interview as he is brooding over his life sentence and seems unable to handle his incarceration.

March 19, 1939

John Couch requests to be placed in the isolation "D" Block.

April 6, 1939

Del Mulcahy is interviewed by the FBI at his apartment at 752 Bayard Street in St. Louis. He states that he had been incarcerated with Couch in the Missouri State Penitentiary. However, he had little contact with him in St. Louis in the Summer of 1938, other than seeing him a few times at the Thomas Tavern on Taylor and Page in St. Louis (which is near Jim's Café). Mulcahy believes he may have seen Meredith there as well on at least one occasion.

April 15, 1939

Peggy Gross marries Sewell Pangman.

June 1, 1939

3:00 p.m.

While in "A" Block, during the evening meal, John Couch stabs inmate George Sink, inmate #414, in the back. He used a weapon fashioned out of a piece of bed slat sharpened on the concrete of the cellblock floor. Sink returns one blow to Couch before the fight is stopped.

Couch is again placed in solitary confinement with restricted diet and loss of privileges until further orders.

June 5, 1939

Couch is removed from solitary confinement to an isolation cell with continued loss of privileges.

June 12, 1939

John Couch gets out his tablet and pencil and writes the following letter to Warden James A. Johnston:

warden

dont think for a minit you and your guards are fooling this chap. I knowed from the beginning what you were up to but you may as well stop your laughing and treat me right and stop telling the other prisoners not to have anything to do with me. Yes a fine warden you are. I guess you will try to feed me some poison if I continue to eat your choice foods. But you are going to get another disappointment. I would rather starve to death than give you and your slave drivers the satisfaction of watching me being eaten up by degrees.

Im writing you just to let you know that I was supposed to have been killed instead of Jack and dont think you can slip one on me by pretending to feed me good choice food. You have already try to get the someone to kill me but that didn't work either and Ill be ready

JUNE 39

warden

dont think for a munit you and your
guards are fooling this chap. I knowed
from the beginning what you were up
to But you may as well stop your laught
in a and treat me right and stop telling
the other prisoners not to have anything
to do with me. yes a fine warden you
are I guess you will try to feed me
some poison if I continue to eate
your choice foods But you are going to
get another disappointment I would
rather starve to death than give you and
your slave drivers the satisfaction of
watching me being eaten up by degrees

Im writing you just to let you know
that I was supposed to have been killed
instead of Jack and dont think you can slip
on me by pretending to feed me good choice
food you have already try to get the someone to
kill me but that didnt work either and Ill be ready

for the next one you send out to get me. He was just lucky and the Gods surely was on his side are else the knife wouldn't have bent. I know how he his been writing you letters and telling you how he is going to feed me glass. He has betrayed your confidence and told me all about your plans against me. All the rest of them is praying to god and I guess you are to but I refuse to let you kill me. I never did you any harm and I didn't rape that girl. get my brother life either. you did said I did and you even had the prisoners to hold that over my head for an excuse to do away with me. I know you had me brought out here for that purpose so I couldn't tell anyone how I am being mistreated. but just remember that when I go I will take my attacker with me. I guess that why they try to sneak up behind me some day I might get a visit and then we will get this thing straighten out. you know who I am. Couch

for the next one you send out to get
me he was just lucky and the Gods
surely was on his side are else the knife
wouldn't have bent I know how he his
been writing you letters and telling you
how he is going to feed me glass he has
betrayed your confidence and told me
all about your plans against me
all the rest of them is praying to god
and I guess you are to but I refuse to
let you kill me I never did you any
harm and I didn't rape that girl get
my brother life either you did said I
did and you even had the prisoners to
hold that over my head for an excuse
to do away with me I know you had me
brought out here for that purpose so
I couldnt tell anyone how I am being
mistreated but just remember that
when I go I will take my attacter
with me I guess that why they try to
sneak up behind me some day I might get
a visit and then we will get this thing
straighten out you know who I am Couch

June 22, 1939

The Neuro-Psychriatic Board at Alcatraz finds that, *"John Couch, #468-AZ, is suffering from a definite Psychosis of a Paranoid nature, which will probably be progressive. He has auditory hallucinations and somatic delusions, believing that serious changes are taking place in his body. He feels he has been put on the spot, and his every thought and action are known to his enemies."*

It is decided that John should be transferred to the Medical Center for Federal Prisoners at Springfield, Missouri.

July 13, 1939

John Couch is transferred from Alcatraz to the MCFP in Springfield, Missouri.

Orders are written to keep Couch in custody there, *"until the prisoner is restored to sanity or health, or until the maximum sentence, without deduction for good time or commutation of sentence, shall have been served."*

APPENDIX

"GANG BUSTERS" Radio Program

"Gang Busters" radio program #287, "The Case of Meredith & Couch," aired nationwide on Friday, November 13, 1942.

Harry Lamson, Jr., son of the Deputy Sheriff who aided in the capture of Couch and Meredith, recalls listening to the show with his father. He says that quite a few liberties were taken with the storyline.

No copies of the script or recording of this episode are known to exist.

DANIEL COX FAHEY, Jr.

Daniel Cox Fahey, Jr. married Virginia McBlair Garesche, a debutante of St. Louis, on November 27, 1938. This marriage did not last very long.

In 1941, Daniel married Katharine Bernays of St. Louis.

They had two daughters, Lucey born in 1942, and Wendy born in 1946.

Fahey was a Colonel in the Army during World War II and received the Legion of Merit while serving with the Operations Division of the War Department's General Staff.

Fahey received a second Legion of Merit for outstanding service as planner for Far Eastern and Pacific matters. He was a key figure in the formulation of policies concerning the administration of civil affairs and military government in the Pacific and Far Eastern theaters.

Fahey was a civilian advisor for the Army for two years following the war.

He received the Eli E. Nobleman Award, "For Outstanding Contributions in the Field of Civil Affairs"

Daniel Cox Fahey, Jr.
Receiving the Legion of Merit

for his civilian aid to the Army, on December 7, 1952.

Fahey was also Director of the National Security Resources Board's Plan Division in Washington as a special management consultant for the Secretary of the Army; Vice-President of Washington Industrial Research Consultants; and a management, financial and international trade consultant for several Washington based organizations.

Fahey was a member of the Metropolitan Club in Washington D.C., the Casanova Hunt Club in Virginia, and was honorary secretary of the Fairfax Hunt.

Daniel Cox Fahey, Jr. died September 1, 1983, in Chevy Chase, Maryland.

VIOLA CECELIA "PEGGY" GROSS

Peggy Gross

Peggy Gross married Carlisle Sewell Pangman on April 15, 1939.

They had one child, Hope, in 1945.

Sewell worked in advertising and marketing.

They resided in St. Louis.

Peggy died June 26, 1974.

VERA MEREDITH

Vera and Howard Siats

Vera Meredith, Jack's wife, married Chiropractor Howard T. Siats on April 21, 1944, in Sioux City, Iowa.

They lived on the Iron Range in Northeastern Minnesota, where most of the Rootes family settled after moving from Effie.

Vera died April 25, 1996, in Hibbing, Minnesota.

DELORIS MARIE MEREDITH

Deloris and Hilton Wollin

Deloris Meredith, Jack and Vera's daughter, married Hilton Clarence Wollin in Hibbing, Minnesota, on March 28, 1952.

They lived on Minnesota's Iron Range, and had five Children.

Deloris passed away March 24, 1985.

IRVIN BURGARD

Irvin Burgard, the 15 year old boy who shot his mother the same night, and near the same area where Couch, Meredith and Reed were traveling with their kidnap victim Robert Kalousek, ran away after the murder and spent four months working for the CCC in Ely, Nevada, under an assumed name.

Irvin Burgard

He was eventually captured and pled guilty to killing his mother.

Before his sentencing, about a dozen witnesses, mostly family members, testified that after Irvin's father died when he was twelve, he was pulled out of school to take over all of the duties of running the farm.

His extremely conservative mother did not allow him to associate with his friends, go to the movies or other activities outside the home, or to even read the funny papers. The witnesses pointed out that Irvin had never been in any other trouble and they doubted he would ever have committed such an act if he had not been brought into such extreme conditions.

The Judge sentenced young Burgard to 15 years in the Missouri State Penitentiary, saying that if he had not received such support from family and neighbors, that he most likely would have been sentenced to life.

Irvin was eventually released, married and raised a family, and died September 5, 1993.

GEORGE COUCH

John Couch's brother George, who was serving a life sentence in the State Prison in Jefferson City, Missouri, for killing a St. Louis Police Officer, stabbed fellow inmate Bremen Riddle on December 22, 1944.

Bremen died from his wounds the following day.

George Thomas Couch was killed with a shiv by another inmate in the prison yard of the Missouri State Penitentiary on October 10, 1953. He was stabbed in the heart.

There were hundreds of other prisoners in the yard playing baseball, basketball, and other games while the stabbing occurred. All continued on with their recreation as normal when Couch fell to the ground.

Warden Ben Stewart said that George Couch was definitely incorrigible, and not a trustworthy prisoner, and that he spent a lot of time in solitary confinement.

DOROTHY COUCH WHITTER

John Couch's sister, having divorced from Arthur Whitter, married John's friend from prison, Delmar Mulcahy, on December 22, 1939.

Dorothy, John's biggest supporter. died May 9, 2007.

PERCY E. FOXWORTH

Assistant FBI Director Percy E. Foxworth, who handled the initial communications on the capture of Couch and Meredith while FBI Director Hoover was away in New York, was eventually assigned as Assistant Director of the New York City Field Office and then Chief of the FBI's Secret Intelligence Service.

Foxworth was killed in a plane crash on January 15, 1943 near Paramaribo, Surinam (then Dutch Guiana) in South America. He was on a secret mission to North Africa to investigate an American citizen alleged to have collaborated with the Nazi's when they controlled North Africa.

The plane crashed due to mechanical problems. Thirty-five people were on board, but virtually no remains were recovered from the debris field, which spread out over a mile.

In his honor, US Naval Liberty Ship S.S. P. E. Foxworth was launched on February 1943.

Foxworth was awarded the FBI Medal of Honor posthumously in the 1991.

HURON TED WALTERS

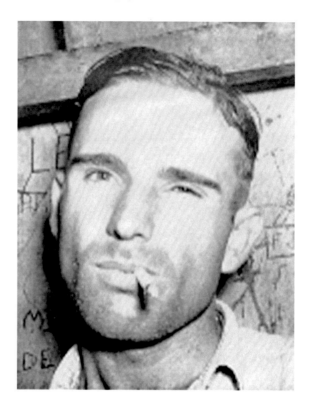

Huron Ted Walters

Huron Ted Walters was sent to Alcatraz from Leavenworth in 1940.

On August 7, 1943, Walters escaped from the prison laundry building but was caught at the shoreline.

After he was released from Alcatraz, he continued his life of crime, being charged with various offenses.

On October 14, 1971, while on the run from an attempted arrest the night before in Euless, Texas, Walters abducted the Hoyt Houston family of Bedford, Texas, in their home.

The Houston's oldest daughter, Pamela, was able to escape through a window and notified authorities.

When the police arrived, Walters forced the Houston family into their car. With a shotgun aimed at Mr. Houston's head from the back seat, Walters forced the officers to drop their weapons while they made a getaway. Authorities forced the vehicle to a stop near Grapevine, Texas, about 300 feet from where Bonnie and Clyde and Henry Methvin had killed two police officers in 1934.

As officers worked to distract Walters, Texas Ranger Tom Arnold took aim on him from behind the car. When Walters moved his shotgun away from Houston's head for a moment, Arnold was able to fire a shot, instantly killing Walters. The Houston family escaped the car uninjured.

FLOYD GARLAND HAMILTON

Floyd Hamilton

Floyd Hamilton was sent to Leavenworth in 1938. In 1940 both he and Huron Ted Walters were transferred to Alcatraz because they were alleged to have been involved in planning an escape.

On April 14, 1943, Floyd Hamilton, James Boarman, Harold Brest and Fred Hunter took two guards hostage in the Industries area. The four climbed out a window and made their way down to the water's edge. One of the guards was able to alert other officers to the escape, and shots were fired at Boarman, Brest and Hamilton, who were all swimming away from the island. Hunter and Brest were both apprehended. Boarman was hit by gunfire and sank before the officers could reach him. His body was never recovered.

Hamilton was initially presumed drowned, but after hiding out for two days in a small shoreline cave, he made his way back up to the Industries area, where he was discovered by officers.

After his escape attempt, Hamilton decided that his best chance at getting out was by being a model prisoner.

After twelve years in Alcatraz, he was transferred back to Leavenworth where he served another six years.

After his release from Leavenworth, he was transferred back to Texas to serve out state charges.

While in prison Floyd studied law, which eventually helped him get his own release, and to assist others in prison who had not received fair trials.

An IQ test administered at his parole hearing showed that Hamilton scored better than 96% of the general public.

Hamilton gained his freedom on July 2, 1958.

W. O. Bankston, a Dallas car dealer, took Hamilton under his wing and gave him a job.

Hamilton started an organization called Conaid, whose mission was to help convicts make a new start. He assisted over 1200 convicts with this organization.

Floyd Hamilton received a Presidential Unconditional Federal Pardon on December 23, 1966, from President Lyndon B. Johnson, and a Texas State Pardon from Governor John Connolly on April 4, 1967. With these pardons, his civil rights were restored.

Floyd remarried his ex-wife Mildred. They had first married in 1929, but had divorced while he was in prison.

Floyd Garland Hamilton died July 24, 1984 in Grand Prairie, Texas, just a few months after the death of his wife Mildred.

JAMES CLYDE REED

James Clyde Reed was born around 1912 to Lawrence Monroe Reed and Alice Christine Brown Reed of St. Louis.

The 1920 Census shows that James and his brother Thomas may have been residents of Father Dunne's Newsboys Home, a Catholic charity in St. Louis providing foster care for boys ages16-21

According to Ancestry.com, James is a direct 8th generation grandson of the explorer Henry Hudson.

No information has been found on James Clyde Reed after his 1938 robbery conviction.

JOHN COUCH

May 5, 1943

John Couch, under maximum custody at the Medical Center for Federal Prisoners in Springfield, Missouri, has just completed a trial period in which he was under just close custody. He had been a custodial and disciplinary problem since being transferred here in 1939. It is decided to try a change of custody from maximum to close.

October 9, 1953

John Couch's parole date comes…and goes.

John Couch

September 8, 1963

John Couch writes a letter to his sister Dorothy.

From: John Couch   *Date: 9-8-63*
To: Mrs Dorothy Couch   *752 Beynard St.*

*Dear sis just a few lines to let you here from me and I hope
you know that you give me a visit telling the people that he
offers me a home and I am asking you to come and see me But
you might no that thay give me some things here that the
mighty god must fight to keep an them footes that I must have
strong foot to hold what thay give to you my food and friend
ship but when you come to see us have some thing to help your
self. I am doing all Right and I hope you will come to see me
some day thay give you a home but you have to fight to keep
that home so be careful for I understand it was hard to keep
things that you want I will close wishing to see some of you
soon*
         Your Brother John

From _John Couch_   9-8-63
                                              (Date)

To _mrs Dorothy couch_   _752 Beynard St._
     (Name)   (Address)

Dear Sis just a few lines to let you here from
me and I hope you know that you give me a visit
tilling the people that he offers me a home and
I am asking you to come and see me But you
might no that thay give me some things here
that the mighty god must fight to keep on
them footes that I must have strong foot
to hold what thay give to you my good and
friend ship but when you come to see us
have some thing to help your self I am doin
all Right and I hope you will come too se
me some day thay give you a home but
you have to fight to keep that home so
be careful for I understand it was hard
to keep things that you want I will close
wisshing to see some of you soon.
       Your Brother John

December 4, 1963

Staff Psychiatrist Alan H. Milofsky at the Medical Center for Federal Prisoners writes to John's sister, Dorothy Mulcahy, requesting permission to renew electro-convulsive therapy on him.

It has been ten years since his last shock therapy, which yielded some positive results.

John is very depressed, not eating regularly, is incoherent, and is not getting along with others.

Dorothy declines, stating that she feels that she cannot make this decision for John.

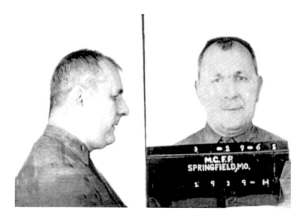

John Couch 1965

November 4, 1970

John Couch is written up for the infraction of "Unauthorized Meat."

While the other inmates were enjoying creamed salmon, John was found with a pork chop on his tray.

Couch admits his guilt. He states that, "Sheema, the white boy," gave him the meat at the salad table.

Infraction noted. No further action taken.

1973

John Couch's medical files show that he is being administered 25 mg of Prolixin every two weeks, and is given 100 mg of Thorazine four times daily. These are antipsychotic drugs used in the treatment of schizophrenia and bipolar disorder, and are being administered at or above the maximum recommended dosages

In July, Couch is interviewed to determine the possibility of releasing him to another facility such as a halfway house.

Couch's sister, Dorothy Mulcahy, expresses an interest in offering her home to John, but she is now a widow on a fixed income, and will have a difficult time supporting him.

It is determined that it is not feasible to transfer John out of the Medical Center for Federal Prisoners at this time.

June 1, 1978

John Couch is again evaluated for fitness to be released from Medical Center for Federal Prisoners in Springfield. The recommendation states:

Couch has been incarcerated for almost 40 years as a result of the serious crime of violence. Although relatively young when first incarcerated on the instant offense, he has grown to be an old man while in prison. He does not appear to be physically or mentally capable of caring for himself if released at this time. Therefore, would need continued institutionalization following release. It is unlikely that he would ever be a threat to society as far as crime and violence is concerned. However, to put him back into society, a life he has never really known, might be even more disturbing to him than remaining in prison surroundings for the rest of his life.

September 21, 1978

John Couch's sister, Dorothy, writes a letter to the Medical Center inquiring about John's mental and physical condition.

Dorothy offers her home to John, but she is concerned whether she can take care of him on her limited income. She is willing to share as much as possible. Case Manager Robert E. Glover replies to Dorothy stating that John has declined some recently but is in about the same condition that he was a couple of years earlier when Dorothy had last visited him.

Glover adds that the staff and other inmates have taken a liking to John and are very protective of him. He seldom communicates verbally with them, but they have developed a type of silent communication with him, and a sort of sixth sense in understanding of him. Physically speaking he is doing well for his age.

August 6, 1979

John Couch writes a letter to the Springfield News-Leader newspaper stating his desire to be free. He says that the Parole Board told him he needed to set up a program to see if he could adjust to society after being in prison for so long. He says that he knows of employees at the Medical Center who would be willing to take him on a furlough for a few hours.

"I have put in a request to the team that I have been assigned to here at the Medical Center for a short furlough. The team heard my request and approved it."

John Couch
1979

His request, along with the approval of his team, were sent to the warden. His request was denied and no reason has been given.

"I do not intend to cause anyone any problems and most of all embarrass anyone who is really trying to help me. If not given the opportunity to see if I can adjust to society, then I would like to know what one in my position has to do to try regain his freedom, what may be left of it."

August 15. 1979

John Couch types a letter to Vice-President Walter
Mondale requesting a pardon:

8,15,1979

To Vice President Mondale,

Vice President Of The United States Of America

Letter For Full Pordon   From President Jimmy Carter,
************************************   *White House*

****

Dear President Mondale,

*My name is John Couch, I have been
in prison 40 years now? I have suffered,And wan/t to live my
last few years at home with my sister? I am not in the best of
health of these last years, Could you please HELP me, I pray
for a PORDON from our President Mr Carter, Would you
please give this letter to him for me, I know Mr Carter must be
a verry bussy man, I do PRAY that you will help me, My sister
is old like myself, She can not do to much. I hope to hear from
the White House soon.*

Mr John Couch

Box 4000

Springfield, Mo

(signature)

8,15,1979
To Vice President Mondale,
Vice President Of The United States Of America

Letter For Full Pordon   From President Jimmy Carter,
*** White House
****

Dear President Mondale,

                    My name is John Couch,i have been in prison
40 years now? I have suffered,And wan/t to live my last few years
at home with my sister? I am not in the best of health of these
last years, Could you please HELP me, I pray for a PORDON from
our President Mr Carter, Would you please give this letter to him
for me,I know Mr Carter must be a verry bussy man,I do PRAY that
you will help me,My sister is old like myself,She can not do to
much. I hope To hear from the White House soon.

                    Mr John Couch
                    Box 4000
                    Springfield,Mo
                    John Couch

September 23, 1979

Reporter Randy Sissel of the Springfield News-Leader writes a front-page article about John Couch's quest for freedom titled, "Inmate Wants Out After 40 Years."

Sissel writes about the recent pardon of several foreign nationals who were serving life sentences for shooting into the US House of Representatives in 1954, wounding five congressman; and another pardon granted to a foreign national who had attempted to assassinate former President Harry Truman in 1950.

He then tells of John Couch, who has been serving a kidnapping sentence since the late 1930s, who can't even get a short furlough off the Medical Center's grounds.

Couch has been turned down for parole at every hearing since he first became eligible in 1953.

The one person who has championed Couch's cause is his sister Dorothy, who has been asking authorities to free her brother for several years.

Sissel was denied access to interview Couch personally, but his interviews with employees of the Medical Center (who remained unnamed) said that they thought short furloughs for Couch would be a good first step.

In a letter dated August 6, 1979, to the News-Leader, Couch wondered what one in his position could do to regain his freedom. Medical Center officials would not answer that question for reporter Sissel.

Dorothy Mulcahy would like to hire an attorney to help her brother, but cannot afford it on her fixed income.

"Johnny has said that he would be willing to eat bologna every day if he could get out," Mrs. Mulcahy said. "He looks so forward to getting out, then they turn him down. I call that toying with somebody's life. I wouldn't blame him to give up, because there is nothing to hold onto."

Employees at the Medical Center, however, say that Couch hasn't given up hoping. He keeps to himself and counts the days until his next parole hearing in July 1980.

Medical Center spokesman John McGathlin said officials must consider the security factor, the inmate's mental state and the type of offender he is when considering a furlough.

McGathlin said he did not know whether Couch was dangerous.

"He is 64 years old. There is no way in the world he could be dangerous," an employee said. "There is no way, especially with two men guarding him. They give the other guys a break. I think he deserves one."

Except for a few walks around the prison yard and the transfer from Alcatraz, Couch has not been outside prison walls for four decades.

John's sister Dorothy said that he had his first brushes with the law in St. Louis when he was a teenager.

She said her brother had problems in school and refused to attend. He was sent to training school at Boonville when he was 12, but he kept running away.

A few years later, he was sent to the state prison in Jefferson City for five years. After he got out, he met up with James Otis Meredith and the two went on a crime spree, eventually kidnapping a St. Louis couple and releasing them in Minnesota. Shortly after they were found by the FBI and Meredith was gunned down trying to escape.

"Many times he has said he wished it was him and not his friend that got machine-gunned down," Mrs. Mulcahy said. "In my heart, I know he hasn't been all that bad. He hasn't deserved that kind of punishment."

She said it seems Medical Center officials are trying to make an example of her brother, "I never could understand why they keep him so long."

January 7, 1980

Case Manager J. R. Linton writes a progress report for John Couch's parole hearing.

He states that because of John's age and condition, it is unlikely that he will ever be a threat to society again.

John feels very strongly about his release, and that he does not want to die in prison.

Linton notes that he is concerned about freeing John into society when he does not handle changes within the institution well. John sometimes refuses food and medication, but when confronted with changing his ward of residence, he will immediately resume normal activity. Based on this, the psychiatric team feels it would be an even greater shock to turn him out into society, and they feel he would be better served staying in Springfield, where he has many friends among the inmate population and staff. However, it is the unanimous decision of the team that John be given a chance to live with his sister in his remaining days. If not with his sister, possibly with a chronic care nursing home.

The psychiatric teams recommends that John receive an effective parole in 1980 with a mental health aftercare condition.

April 1, 1980

George A. Ralston, Jr., Warden of US MCFP, writes to Community Programs Officer James L. Jones, regarding placing John Couch in a Community Treatment Center upon his parole of April 21, 1938.

Initial placement in a Community Treatment Center is a condition of his parole. Couch is not employable, and cannot apply for Social Security benefits while incarcerated. The Community Treatment Center would allow time to align some sort of subsistence such as S.S.I. or welfare, as well as a structured reintegration into society.

Ralston notes that Couch is in need of close supervision for purposes of his own personal hygiene and sanitation, in that he must be told to shower and shave.

Couch also begs for coffee and cigarettes from other inmates, who usually give him these items. Over the years, Couch has become a pet that staff and inmates have pampered.

Ralston states that John Couch eventually plans on living with his sister, Dorothy, in Ballwin, Missouri. He also states that Mr. Eldon Cobb, Laundry Foreman at US MCFP, has offered to escort John Couch to the Community Treatment Center.

April 8, 1980

    Dismas House of Saint Louis, a Community Treatment Center, agrees to accept John Couch upon his parole of April 21, 1980.

John Couch 1980

April 21, 1980

    John Couch receives a parole
    John has gotten along reasonably well the past few years. He was living in an open psychiatric unit, but did not venture off the ward very often.

He is still on Prolixin. He has a rather severe case of emphysema, but refuses to take treatment for it. He has a tendency to get uptight and hyperventilate, but can be calmed down to recover.

John is hoping to eventually move in with his sister Dorothy.

Eldon Cobb, the laundry foreman at the Medical Center, escorts John to Dismas House.

Couch is given $100 spending money.

May 19, 1980

John Couch is transferred from Dismas House to the Pine Crest Adult Boarding Facility in Ballwin, Missouri. This is within walking distance of his sister Dorothy's house. John frequents a local ice cream stand almost daily.

John Couch and sister Dorothy 1980

F. L. Zimmerman, Executive Director of Dismas House, writes to Community Programs Officer Jim Jones that John Couch has settled into Pine Crest, and that, "All is well. Because of your persistence, he is happy in freedom."

Dorothy is not pleased with Pine Crest. It is crowded, unclean and not particularly safe. She is appreciative of what they are doing for John, but would like to find another facility for him. John seems to enjoy Pine Crest just fine.

Arthur Whitter and John Couch 1984

Dorothy is eventually able to place John at the Sunrise Nursing Home in Union, Missouri, where he lived until his death as a result of cardiac arrest on July 7, 1984.

John Couch is buried in the Hiram Gardens section of Bellerive Heritage Gardens Cemetery in Creve Coeur, Missouri, Section B, Lot 39, Space 5.

ACKNOWLEDGEMENTS

Chance Anderson – Consulting and assistance
Darcie Anderson - Consulting and assistance
Eva Anderson - Consulting and assistance
Randy Bell - Rich Hill, Missouri historian
Judy Berry - Daughter-in-law to the Berry's
         who owned the Red Onion Café
David Black - Malden, Missouri Historian
Hope Blumeyer- Peggy Gross' Daughter
Mike Brey - Champlin, Minnesota Historian
Kathy Brinkley - State Line Campground photo
William Brown - Hennepin County Surveyor
Lou Burr - Meredith tombstone photo
Jim Byerly - MN Department of Transportation Librarian
Chevy Chase, Maryland Historical Society
Jack Clay -St. Francois, Missouri Historical Society
Kathleen Conway-Friends of Historic Boonville
Ona Coughlin - Metropolitan Club of Washington, DC
Lilah Crowe and Crew - Itasca County Historical Society
Bonnie Drobnik - Itasca County Recorder's Office
Tina Easley - Cole's Hotel Photo
Farmington, Missouri Chamber of Commerce
FBI - Case File
Fort Worth Police Department Historical Association
Tom Finley - Friend of the Faheys
Brian Flakne - Kleve Flakne's Grandson
Kit Foster - Ford car illustrations from kitfoster.com
Cissy Finley Grant – D.C. Columnist
Jamie Hamlin - Fairfax Hunt
Kitty Hartman - Dr. Bender's Daughter
Wayne Herron -James Thomas Meredith's grandson
Historical Society of Washington, DC
Sandra Lee Hockenbury - Couch's grandniece
Dave Johnson - Arlington, Texas Historian
Sandra Knight - Meredith's Niece

Leonard Knotts, Jr. - Effie Historian
Harry Lamson, Jr. - Deputy Lamson's son
Susan Larson-Fleming - Hennepin History Museum
Matthew Lassegard – Ramsey Co. Sheriff's Dept. Historian
Dr. Art Lee- Historian
Wes Libbey - Meredith's Coroner and Mortician
Budge Lund - witnessed FBI arrest from nearby
Eleanor Lynch - Metropolitan Club of Washington, D.C.
Ann McDonald - Malden, MO Historical Society
Colleen McKnight - History Society of Washington DC
Linda McIntosh - Kitchigami Regional Library System
Bart McClaughry - Rich Hill, Missouri historian
Jim Martin - Wildwood, Missouri Historical Society
Pat Maus - Curator of the Northeast MN Historical Center
Shirley Meyers - Editor
Irene Meredith Pfeiffer - Alfred Meredith's wife
Tim Rives - National Archives at Kansas City, Missouri
Terry Romstad - Couch tombstone photo
Randolph Rouse - Fairfax Hunt, friend of
                              Daniel Cox Fahey, Jr.
Joe Sanchez - National Archives at San Bruno, California
Joan Sharpe - CCC Legacy
Doug Shelton - Wakefield Arms information
Pat Snodgrass - Brooklyn Historical Society, Minnesota
Stephen Sokoloff - Dunklin Co. MO Prosecuting Attorney
Barbara Sommer – CCC Historian
Darcy Tiburzi - Meredith's Granddaughter
MC Toyer - Dallas Historian
Jerre Tracy - Historic Fort Worth
Myrleen Watkins-Starkey - Dunklin County Library
Jack White - Fort Worth Historian
Western Itasca Review - Deer River, Minnesota

And my apologies to all of the folks who have helped me out
that I have forgotten to acknowledge here.

1-800-297-2335
"Walk T. T. Com"